The Shack by the Sea

By the same author
LESLIE'S LEAP

Nick Yapp

The Shack by the Sea

HODDER AND STOUGHTON
LONDON SYDNEY AUCKLAND TORONTO

British Library Cataloguing in Publication Data
Yapp, Nick
  The shack by the sea.
  I. Title
  823'.914[J]   PZ7

ISBN 0-340-38806-4

Copyright © Nick Yapp 1987

First published 1987

All rights reserved. No part of this publication may be
reproduced or transmitted, in any form or by any means,
electronic or mechanical, including photocopy, recording,
or any information storage and retrieval system, without
permission in writing from the publishers.

Published by Hodder and Stoughton Children's Books,
a division of Hodder and Stoughton Ltd,
Mill Road, Dunton Green, Sevenoaks, Kent TN13 2YJ

Photoset by Rowland Phototypesetting Ltd,
Bury St Edmunds, Suffolk

Printed in Great Britain by St Edmundsbury Press Ltd,
Bury St Edmunds, Suffolk

Chapter One

It had been a strange week, and Joanne had missed her friends back in London. People were right when they said the seaside was 'dead' out of season, and the October half term was right out of season. There had been the novelty of their new caravan, but novelties don't last long. Especially in cold weather, and today was very cold.

Joanne shivered.

The strong, offshore wind strengthened, whipping the sand off the top of the dunes and across the beach.

Ben moved closer to his sister.

'Are we going to fly my kite? It's a good wind.'

'It's too cold.'

The emptiness of Camber Sands made it seem even colder. Mum and Dad had decided to stay in the car, down in the car park, on the other side of the dunes.

The beach, the whole bay, was deserted. The tide was going out. Narrow channels, miniature estuaries, chased the retreating sea, like children scampering after a grown up.

Joanne stood at the top of the dunes, her hands deep in her anorak pockets, as far away as possible from the biting wind. It seemed a pity to waste the deserted beach. What a place for a daydream!

'We're shipwrecked,' she said. 'We're all alone.'

'Not really,' said Ben. 'Mum and Dad are in the car park.'

'No, they're not. We haven't got a mum and dad. We're shipwrecked orphans. We keep trying to attract the attention of passing ships – but to no avail.'

'To no what?' said Ben.

'There's a ship! Wave!'

'So what,' said Ben. 'There's another one over there. An oil tanker. Going towards Hastings.' He pointed.

Joanne curled her lip. She'd been practising in front of the mirror, and did it quite well now, hardly closing her eye at all.

'You're so boring,' she said. 'You probably don't even realise how boring you are.'

'I do,' said Ben, indignantly.

Joanne took a deep breath, and tried once more.

'Look, there's no one else about, is there? So what's wrong with pretending? We could be orphans.'

'What happened to Mum and Dad?'

'There was a dreadful storm that snapped our boat in half, and everyone was drowned but us.'

'Why were we in a boat?'

'I don't know. We were going to France.'

'Why?'

'To do Christmas shopping. Lynsey's family go to the hypermarket in Boulogne to do Christmas shopping.'

'In October?'

'Yes.'

'Well, why did the ship sink? Storms don't snap ships in half.'

'All right. It hit another boat in the crowded Channel lanes.'

'Why didn't the other boat pick us up?'

'It sank, too.'

'What about lifeboats? All Channel ferries have lifeboats. And if the Channel lanes are so crowded, then we should have been rescued almost as soon as we were shipwrecked.'

'Oh, shut up,' said Joanne.

Ben smiled smugly. Joanne decided not to kick him – such an action would lack the dignity that she should display as a teenager. She walked angrily away.

Ben, who had expected to be kicked, followed her – at a distance.

It would soon be tea-time. The light was beginning to fade. Tomorrow night the clocks would go back an hour, and the second, darker phase of autumn would be upon them.

As she walked along the crest of the dunes, Joanne tried to ignore Ben's presence.

'What about my kite?'

She wondered what it would be like to be an orphan. Glamorous, maybe. Sad, of course. But sort of attractive.

'I thought it was generally agreed that I was to fly my kite this afternoon?'

Hope you trip over your kite string and break your miserable neck, thought Joanne.

'I thought you said we were all alone in the world.'

This time Joanne did respond.

'What do you mean?'

'We're not alone,' said Ben. 'There's him.'

For a moment Joanne couldn't see what he was pointing at. The light was poor. Everything looked grey. She strained her eyes. Then she saw a tiny movement, far out, across the wide sweep of Rye Bay. A man, jogging over the sand, and kicking something.

'He's playing football,' said Ben.

As her eyes got used to the light, Joanne could see more clearly. The man was moving over the wet sand, and kicking a ball in front of him. Although he didn't seem to kick the ball very hard, in the strong wind it was moving rapidly.

The children watched. When he reached the water's edge, the man picked the ball up. To their surprise, he threw it hard and high, out into the sea.

'Stupid thing to do,' said Ben. 'He'll lose it.'

They were both conscious of their father's warnings about the dangers of the offshore wind – don't chase anything being carried out to sea. Well, this bloke certainly wasn't chasing after the football. He stood there, watching it, as the ball skimmed across the water at an astonishing rate. Within a very short time it was out of sight.

'He's had it now,' said Ben. 'Waste of a football.'

He quickly lost interest.

'I want my tea,' he said, and plunged down the inland side of the dunes, heading for the car park.

For a couple of minutes, Joanne stayed where she was. She peered across the sands at the man. He, too, was standing still, gazing out to sea. Then, abruptly, he turned away, and walked briskly back over the sands, heading for the golf course on the western edge of Camber Sands.

It was strange, but was it worth daydreaming about?

Joanne decided it wasn't.

She was wrong.

Chapter Two

In the morning Ben got what he wanted and they went to fly his kite. It suited Mum, it suited Dad, it suited Ben. It suited everyone but Joanne.

Mum was busy cleaning, and Dad was busy making a mess – sawing, sanding, chiselling, fitting shelves and cupboards in their new caravan.

'If you take Ben off,' Mum said to Joanne, 'there's a chance I can clear up round your father.'

'What about Ben's mess?' said Joanne. 'He should clear that up.'

'What mess?' said Ben, stung.

Joanne pointed to the accumulation of bits of crab and rotting seaweed, and chalk and shells, and half-eaten sticks of rock.

'That mess,' she said.

Ben shook his head. 'Valuable,' he said.

'Go on,' said Mum. 'Get out of it. Go and fly your kite. It'll save having a row.'

'There isn't enough wind,' said Joanne.

'Just take him for a walk then,' said Mum.

'A walk!' Ben made it sound as if the NSPCC should hear of this.

Yeah, thought Joanne. Too lazy to clear up and too lazy to go for a walk, but she knew what was expected of her.

'OK, Misery,' she said. 'Let's go to the beach.'

'And I'll take my kite,' said Ben, with a touch of suffering bravely borne in his voice. 'Because you wouldn't let me fly it yesterday.'

Joanne was about to explode. Her mother took hold of her arm.

'Don't be ridiculous, Ben. And don't shrug your shoulders. You're lucky to have an older sister to look after you. You can't expect Joanne to go on doing it much longer. You're old enough to do things for yourself.'

'Exactly,' said Dad, measuring a gap between two cupboard units. 'What I've been saying for some time. Like to give me a hand with this?'

'No, I wouldn't,' said Ben, with fervour. He had helped Dad put up the new garden shed three months ago, and hadn't recovered yet.

Mum turned briskly to Ben. 'If you want to hang about here, I can find some shopping that needs to be done. Stuff to take home for the weekend.'

'All right, all right,' said Ben, grudgingly. 'I'll take my kite for a walk.'

Joanne and Ben left the caravan and walked in silence to the main entrance to the caravan park. Ben had a little money to spend at The Stores. It was Saturday, new comics day. Joanne waited while he made his selection, flicking through the picture magazines of romance and adventure. Romance and adventure! Not at Winchelsea Beach. Not with Ben.

He was waiting at the checkout. She saw him pick up a Mars bar. As they left the shop together she said: 'You're not supposed to buy sweets.'

'Sweets?' said Ben, as though searching in his mind to recall if he'd ever heard that word before.

'Mum reckons you're getting fat.'

'At least I'm not skinny,' said Ben.

She didn't rise to the bait. She was getting less skinny, and she was growing up. He was still a child, and she would soon be an adolescent. It was a nice thought.

And it was going to be a fine day. The sun was shining. It was much warmer than yesterday, but there was hardly any wind. Not a suitable day for flying a kite.

As if reading her thoughts, Ben said: 'Now let's go to fly my kite on the beach.'

Joanne didn't argue. She followed him to the beach, along the path, up the steps, over the sea wall, across the shingle, and down on to the sand.

There wasn't enough wind.

'I'm sure there *is* enough wind,' said Ben, head well down, unravelling his kite-string.

Joanne stood it for a while. Running up and down the sand, throwing the kite into the air and watching the stupid thing flop down. She was glad there was no one else there to witness the sight.

'It won't work,' she said, for the seventh time.

'It nearly did then,' said Ben, also for the seventh time.

'Try on your own,' said Joanne, sweetly.

She sat on the breakwater and watched him. She wasn't sure which bit she enjoyed best: the moment when the kite plummeted on to his head, or when he got the string round his big toe and pulled himself over.

Eventually he gave up.

'Now can we go for a walk?' said Joanne.

'Might as well,' said Ben, moodily.

'And you can eat your Mars bar to give you lots and lots of energy.'

'Are you going to tell?'

'No.'

'Then I won't say anything about your make-up.'

It was a shame nothing exciting ever happened to Ben, thought Joanne. In the past she had hoped gypsies would kidnap him, or pirates, or the press-gang. Now she pinned her hopes on a convenient quicksand.

They walked back up the shingle and climbed on to the sea-wall.

Although the wall was only a little higher than the surrounding land, it gave you views in all directions. To the west was Fairlight, where the land rose and cliffs swung out to the sea. To the north were the towns of Winchelsea and Rye, standing proudly above the flat farmland and the river basin. To the east was the River Rother, and beyond that Camber Sands. To the south was the sea, stretching away to France. Today it was a deep blue, with dark green stumps of breakwater jutting up from it, like the skeletal ribs of wrecked ships. Piled up between the wall and the sea was the yellow and brown and blue mosaic of shingle – hard on the feet, even in shoes, and dotted with patches of oil and tar that drove Mum wild if it got on people's clothes.

They left the sea-wall. Joanne set a brisk pace, along a rough stone track called the Ridgeway, where sharp flints stuck out of the mud, and there were many potholes. Weird, it was here. A mixture of dilapidated huts and little brick bungalows. The whole place had a run-down, abandoned look. There were funny little gardens, some gone to seed, some occupied by weather-beaten gnomes. Here and there were gaps between the buildings, as though flimsier dwellings had been blown away by the storms that lashed in from the sea in winter time. Dad always said it must be bitterly cold in December and January. But most of these places would be empty then, not many of them had year-round residents. In a couple of weeks the whole Ridgeway could well be deserted.

Both children knew the area well. Only the caravan was new to them. They knew about Rye, and its connection with smugglers. They knew Camber Sands, and the Pipewell Gate and the Museum in Winchelsea. Joanne felt the place had little new to offer her.

'Can you carry my kite?' Ben was bleating.

'No.'

'No, I didn't think you could.' Ben's remark ended with a sigh, as though from somewhere he would find a little more saintly patience.

They reached the end of the Ridgeway. Here there was a crossroads. Straight ahead, a cart track passed a series of flooded gravel pits called Nook Beach, on its way to Rye Harbour. To the right a narrow path led back to the sea-wall. To the left was the path to Camber Castle.

Joanne turned left, up a slight rise. They were on the fringe of the largest of the flooded pits – Long Pit, it was called. There were warning signs:

DANGER

DEEP WATER

and:

CHILDREN NOT PERMITTED

WITHIN RESTRICTED AREA

'Nobody seems to want children to have any fun,' said Ben.

'Go in there and the only fun you'll have is drowning.' Joanne toyed with the idea of encouraging him. No, Mum and Dad might be upset.

The path descended, crossed a field of stubble and entered a wood. The trees were thin, spindly. Joanne remembered being told at school that the whole of Sussex had once been a huge forest. This was a poor remnant. There were a few willows, hawthorn, and some stunted holly bushes. Clumps of bramble, elder and fading cow-parsley formed the undergrowth. After the open expanses of sea and sky, even a small wood, such as this, seemed quiet, dark and enclosed.

Joanne was soon through the wood, with Ben straggling further and further behind. The path ran alongside a field of collapsing, dying sweetcorn. At the very edge of the field, growing haphazardly, like weeds, were one or two cabbages, and tomato plants, with clusters of undersized green fruit. The sun would never ripen them now, and soon the frosts would kill both fruit and plants. It seemed odd to see tomato plants so far from any house.

Perhaps some fugitive, ages ago, had tried to grow vegetables here. A fugitive living in a mud hovel in the woods, desperate to remain hidden, coming out only at night – like an urban fox.

It must have been awful to be a fugitive. Completely alone. On the run. The whole country on the lookout for you. Never safe. Never able to seek help. A price on your head, and only the gallows waiting for you.

Joanne's thoughts wandered to more important matters. It was about time she did something with her hair. It was too long. She would have to persuade Mum and Dad to let her try a new style. Vanessa had been allowed to go to London and spend twelve pounds on a haircut. That was living.

'Jo!'

The cry from Ben sounded urgent. Didn't it always?

'Jo! Help!'

She turned. He was sprawled on the path, clutching his leg, rocking to and fro, and almost screaming.

Chapter Three

At first, Joanne assumed Ben was fooling about, pretending.

'What's the matter?' she called back.

No answer. Typical. Frantic beckoning, but no explanation. Joanne stumped back to him, and stood over him, wanting to kick him.

'Someone's shot me in the leg,' he said. 'I expect it's broken.'

'Piffle.'

'Oh, yes?' Ben rolled up the bottom of his jeans. 'Look.'

It was true. On his shin was a blotchy red mark, and the beginnings of a darkening bruise – a bad bruise.

Joanne dropped on her knees beside him. He hadn't been shot, otherwise there'd be masses of blood and she'd have heard the gun. But something had happened.

'How did you do that?' she said, prodding his leg gently.

'Ouch! That hurt! Leave it alone, it's my wound.' Ben pushed her hand away. 'I didn't do it. I tell you, I've been shot.'

'So – where's the bullet?'

'More to the point,' said Ben, 'will I ever walk again?'

'Well, get up and try. Here – hold on to my arm.'

Leaning heavily on his sister, Ben struggled to his feet.

'Ow! It really does hurt.' He sounded quite pleased, and took one or two dramatically faltering steps. 'You'll have to carry me.'

'Fat chance. But how did it happen? You must have fallen over, or banged into something.'

'I tell you, I didn't. I was walking along, thinking about how wonderful it would be if I got a real chance to fly my kite, when "wham!" – something hit me in the leg. Really hard. I reckon it must have been a bullet. And the gun had a silencer on it.'

Joanne was startled by a noise, close by. A noise like a sneeze, or a suppressed snort of laughter. It came from the wood.

Ben was hobbling about, peering at the ground. He had evidently heard nothing. Joanne peered into the wood. It was difficult to see anything through the screen of yellow and brown leaves.

'If it wasn't a bullet, then I bet this is what did it.' Ben had found a sharp edged stone, about the size of a golf-ball, and was holding it against his bruise, to see if it fitted.

Joanne didn't reply. She stood perfectly still, staring into a patch of elder bushes. There wasn't any wind to rustle the leaves, but she was certain she had seen a slight movement.

'Yes,' continued Ben, 'I reckon it's this stone, which means someone bunged it. Someone evil. An evil nitwit.'

There was an immediate response from the elder patch. Twigs cracked underfoot, branches moved furiously, and a figure leapt out.

Ben, taken completely by surprise, fell over, scrambled up and grabbed his sister's hand.

'Who you callin' nitwit?' It was a challenging remark, with more than the hint of a sneer behind it. More breaking of twigs, more swaying of branches, and the figure advanced into the open, and stood facing them.

It was a girl, Joanne reckoned, but not obviously so. Small, with a dirty white face, and black hair that looked as though it could do with a wash. The clothes were rough and ready: T-shirt, jeans and trainers. That much Joanne noticed at a glance. That much, and one thing more. The figure had her right hand raised, and in that hand was a stone, poised, ready to throw.

'Eh? Who you callin' nitwit?'

Ben said nothing. Joanne didn't know what to say.

'You want this? Eh? You want this in your face? It was the leg last time. You can 'ave it in the face, if you like.' The figure took a step forward.

Joanne's throat was dry, her heart was thumping, her mind was racing. What could they do? Run? Couldn't – Ben could hardly walk. Shout for help? There was no one about. Threaten? That didn't seem very wise. Joanne doubted that she was a match for this girl.

Perhaps it would be best to try to ignore the second stone, the one in the hand, and concentrate on the first.

'Why did you throw a stone at my brother?'

A simple question. Joanne meant it to sound unthreatening, like those bits on television when the police talk an armed gangster into giving himself up.

The girl took a step towards them, and raised her right hand an inch or two.

Why couldn't life be more like television!

But nothing was thrown.

'You could have blinded him!'

The girl let her right arm drop, and placed both hands on her hips.

'If I'd wanted to blind 'im, I could 'ave, right? But I didn't want to. I was aimin' at 'is leg, an' I 'it 'is leg. Right? That's 'cos I always 'it what I aim at. An' I'd like to know 'ow you reckon a nitwit could do that.'

'I don't think it's clever to throw stones at people.'

'And why me?' added Ben.

The girl threw the stone back over her shoulder.

'I've got rid of it. Right? It's gone. OK? So jus' don't keep goin' on about it.'

'It's a very bad bruise,' said Ben, holding his leg out towards the girl.

Joanne waited for the girl to say: 'Sorry'.

Ben waited.

And, while they waited, their gaze never left the girl. Birds called. A power-saw roared from a nearby farm. Some dogs barked in the distance. Nobody spoke.

The girl broke the deadlock.

'Hear that?' she said.

'What?'

'Them dogs.'

'Is it bloodhounds?' asked Ben. 'Have you escaped from prison?'

The girl made a face. 'You interested in secrets?' she said.

Joanne didn't answer.

Ben pointed at his sister. 'She is,' he said.

'Right,' said the girl. 'Climb through 'ere an' follow me.'

Without pausing to think, Joanne and Ben crawled under the strands of the wire fence.

The girl led them through the wood. She was clearly making some effort to avoid undue noise, but seemed more concerned not to be seen.

When they came out of the wood, by the flooded gravel pit, the girl stopped and dropped on all fours.

'Keep down. It's best to crawl. Keep yer 'eads down especially.'

'Why? Somebody else chucking stones?' said Ben.

The girl smiled.

They moved slowly, bent double. Ben's kite made progress extremely difficult. Several times the girls had to wait while Ben transferred his kite from one arm to the other, or while he re-coiled its tail.

The girl clearly found this irritating.

'If you can't get a move on, I'll ditch that.'

Ben gave her one of his crushing looks.

'Is 'e goin' to be sick?' asked the girl.

'No, I'm not!' said Ben, indignantly.

'Well, do somethin' to your face before I do,' said the girl.

They hurried on. It was hard, breathless work, and there was no time for Ben to give vent to his sense of outrage. Whatever the secret was, the girl was clearly in a hurry to reveal it to them.

After a quarter of a mile or so, the girl headed south, towards the sea. Here the gravel pits narrowed into separate channels, fringed with reeds. They were on a pinched neck of land, with water on either side. The girl lay down, close to the water, and signalled that they were to do the same. Ben flopped down and began to smoothe out his kite, which had suffered almost as much as he had during their journey.

Joanne licked her lips and wished that she had something to drink. She wondered what they were waiting for. Something to happen? Somebody to arrive?

The girl's thin finger poked her in the ribs.

'Listen,' whispered the girl.

Joanne listened. There was little to hear. The occasional slap of water. The mewing of gulls. Rustling of grass. And the dogs, louder and nearer.

Joanne frowned. 'I can't hear anything,' she said.

The girl nodded vigorously, as if to say: 'Oh, yes, you can'.

'I'm bored,' said Ben.

'Shut yer face,' hissed the girl.

It worked wonders.

The sound of the barking was coming from a cluster of farm buildings on the other side of the cart track. Around the buildings were rusting pieces of farm machinery, bales of fading straw and stacks of damp wood. The place had a derelict air.

The barking continued.

The girl was peering at Joanne's face, as if waiting for light to dawn.

'Listen!' The girl's voice was insistent.

Joanne listened. The girl pointed to the barns.

Nothing – just the tinny barking of dogs coming from some empty farm buildings. No one about. No movement.

At last Joanne realised what the girl was getting at. It didn't make sense. It didn't fit. The dogs barking all the time, when there was nothing to disturb them.

The girl nodded.

'Nutty, innit,' she said. 'No one about, an' them dogs carryin' on as though they was in the middle of a fox-hunt. An' I'll tell you somethin' else.'

Joanne was hooked. Even Ben was listening now.

'No dogs.'

Joanne stared at her.

'It's a tape-recordin'. Goes on and on. Bloke comes along sometimes an' switches it off.'

'How do you know?'

'Seen 'im. Been over there, too. That shed. Door's locked, but you can see a bit through the window. Dark in there. Creepy. Rats. But there ain't no dogs. Bits of wire, an' a tape-recorder, an' this bloke goes there to change the batt'ries.'

'What's it all for?'

'Dunno. Good secret, though. Mus' be up to somethin'. An' that dog noise is to drive noseys away. There's notices, too, near the barns. In case some bold nutter thinks she'll 'ave a go at sussin' it out. "Guard Dogs Patrolling". Didn't keep me out.'

The girl smiled.

'There's someone coming.' Ben was the first to notice a motor-bike coming from the direction of Rye Harbour.

The girl grabbed his arm.

'Get down!' she ordered.

Joanne and Ben flattened themselves on the ground. It was difficult to see through the grasses and reeds, but they could hear the motor-bike stop. Joanne risked raising her head a little. She saw the rider dismount and look about him.

'Checkin' to see that no one's watchin',' said the girl, quietly, but smugly.

The man unlocked the door of the shed and went inside. A few moments later the barking stopped abruptly.

'There you are,' said the girl. ''E's turned it off. To change the batt'ry. Like muckin' out the stables. But not so messy.'

Joanne looked at Ben's watch. Ten past eleven. They had plenty of time.

'Shall we wait?' she said to the girl. 'See what happens?'

'Course.'

Joanne was beginning to enjoy herself. They'd got off to a funny start, but there was no reason why they shouldn't be friends. The problem would be Ben. He wasn't any good at waiting.

Minutes passed. Ben became fidgety.

'How much longer? I want to fly my kite.'

'You'll have to blow 'ard. Ain't no wind.'

'I'm hungry.'

'Bite yer fingernails.'

Her sarcasm silenced him, and he wriggled backwards, away from the two girls.

'Got the 'ump,' said the girl, cheerfully.

She and Joanne kept watch on the barns. There was the motor-bike, gleaming in the autumn sunshine. The man had made no attempt to hide it.

Ben wriggled further away.

After a few minutes the barking restarted. Then the door of the shed opened, and the man emerged, carrying something under his arm. He placed the 'something' in his pillion-bag, and strapped on his crash-helmet. He swung his leg over the saddle.

Joanne waited, expecting to see him turn the bike round and head back towards Rye Harbour.

But the man suddenly stood up, legs straddling the saddle, and stared in the children's direction.

'Where's your brother?' the girl whispered, urgently.

Joanne glanced behind her. To her horror, there was Ben, fifty metres away, between the narrow channels of water, in full view, throwing his wretched kite into the air, in a stupid and totally hopeless attempt to make it fly.

'Ben!'

But he was too far away to hear.

Joanne switched her gaze back to the barns. The man was looking at Ben.

'Ben! Get down!' It was as near a shout as she dared, but it was too little and too late.

She heard the engine roar as the man kicked the bike into life. She saw the wheels spin on a patch of shingle. The man was off – and not towards Rye. He clearly wanted to get to Ben.

But there was a barbed-wire fence between him and the children. He would have to find a way round this, and, until he did so, they had a chance to get away.

The girl sprang into action.

She leapt up, and raced across to Ben, shouting as she did so.

''Ere, loony – quick as you can! Follow me!'

Joanne plunged after her, grabbing Ben's hand as she ran past him.

It was the beginning of a strange, wild chase – terrifying and totally incomprehensible. They seemed to be heading randomly to and fro, like rats scurrying in a maze. Sometimes the motor-cyclist was in front of them, on the other side of a channel of water. Sometimes he was behind them, travelling across their path. To anyone watching, the whole thing might have looked ridiculously funny, like some mad race. To those taking part it was very serious. Joanne could see that the girl who had led them into this mess wasn't wasting any time. She was running flat out, and urging Ben and Joanne to keep up with her.

Occasionally Joanne shot a glance at their pursuer. She could see his arms, his legs and his body, but she couldn't see his face. He wore a dark, perspex visor, pulled down from his helmet. Where his face should have been there was a blank, dark space – empty and menacing. It was like something out of *Star Wars* – Darth Vader on a motor-bike. Black boots, black jeans, black jacket, black helmet.

Ben, encumbered by his kite, suddenly panted: 'Can't we stop and explain?'

'Shift yerself,' said the girl.

Explain?

Joanne wondered what they were supposed to explain. There was nothing to explain. They had done nothing wrong. They hadn't been trespassing. They hadn't stolen anything. They hadn't damaged anything. They had merely been listening. You couldn't get into trouble just for listening – could you?

As she stumbled along, she recalled that secrets always lead to trouble. That was why everyone got so excited about them. There was always something dangerous in a secret. And there was something decidedly dangerous about the look of the man on the motor-bike.

But Ben couldn't keep going much longer.

'Done 'im!'

There was triumph in the girl's voice. She stopped, and pointed back. Joanne's chest was heaving, and her breath was coming in great gulps. Her teeth were aching with the effort of breathing. She looked back. The motor-bike was much farther away than she had expected, than she had feared.

''E's got lost. Took a wrong turn. Got to find 'is way out. Still, don't do to 'ang about.'

The girl hurried on, but not at the breakneck speed she had set originally.

They had returned to the restricted area, back to the DANGER sign. The three children scrambled under the wire fence and plunged into the wood. The girl clearly knew where she was taking them. They left the path, squeezed between the brambles, and came out into a small clearing in the middle of the wood.

And there, tucked away in the corner, was a railway carriage.

''Ere we are,' said the girl. 'Welcome to the 12.34 from London Bridge. 'Op in quick, before the guard blows 'is whistle.'

She opened one of the carriage doors and shoved them both inside.

Chapter Four

'And where do you think she's gone?' said Annie.

'How should I know!' Carol stared out of the window.

'You're supposed to be her best mate. I should have thought you'd know.'

'Well, I don't. She never told *me* she was going.'

They were in the kitchen of the children's home. Annie, the weekend cook, was doing what she was paid to do. Carol was leaning on the window-frame and gazing at the back garden. It was a large garden, surrounded by a mournful mass of evergreen shrubs. The early-morning fog had lifted, and a weak sun was beginning to shine on the glistening leaves.

'Not surprised she ran away,' said Carol. 'Miserable hole, this is.'

'Where is everyone today?' asked Annie.

'Gone off.'

'Where to?'

'Macdonald's.'

'I hope Mr Flaskett doesn't expect me to cook for a load of children that have had their appetites spoiled.'

'It's all right,' said Carol. 'They've only gone for a snack. Jim wanted them out of the way.'

'Didn't he want you out of the way?'

'Me?' Carol gave Annie a huge smile. 'He relies on me.'

'Why did he want the others out of the way, then?'

'There's this meeting. About Sharon. Jim reckons she's made a lot of trouble for him.'

'I should think she has! Silly little madam. Running off like that. She must have said *something*!'

Annie was banging about the kitchen, preparing vegetables.

'It's not the first time,' she said.

'No.'

'Who's coming to this meeting?'

'Social workers. The Graingers.'

'The people that are going to foster Sharon?' Annie started to chop onions.

'Not if Sharon has her way.'

'I'd have thought she'd jump at the chance. Home of her own.'

'You seen the Graingers?'

'Too fussy by half, Sharon,' said Annie.

The door opened. Jim Flaskett came in. Tall, strong, and, as a rule, bossy. But he looked tired this morning, and there was a distinct stoop about his shoulders.

'Hallo, Annie,' he said.

'Not found her yet, then?' said Annie.

'Not yet.' He picked up a piece of raw carrot. Annie made as if to smack his hand, but took one look at his face and checked herself.

Jim swallowed his carrot. 'It would help if we knew where to look.' He scratched his forehead, as if his thoughts, like Sharon, were miles away. 'Can we have some coffee for the meeting, Annie?'

'How many cups?'

'Eight. And some chocolate biscuits, if we've got

them. Nothing like chocolate for putting everyone in a good mood.'

'Your Sharon took the last of the chocolate biscuits with her when she went. Three packets.'

Jim groaned.

'Have we got any other biscuits?'

'A few very old digestives.'

'They'll do. They'll have to.' Jim looked at Carol. 'Can you bring the coffee and biscuits in when it's ready? And do it ever so nicely, Carol, won't you? Please?'

Carol smiled. 'I'll make sure you're ever so proud of me,' she said. 'Shall I curtsey?'

Jim pulled a face and went out.

Carol started to arrange cups, saucers and spoons on a tray.

'Sharon ran off on Wednesday night, didn't she?' asked Annie.

'Or early Thursday morning. Jim's not sure.'

'Been gone a long time, then. How did she get out?'

'Through the window. Jim found it open Thursday morning. He thinks she must have climbed down the creeper outside. Bed hadn't been slept in.'

'Might have killed herself,' said Annie.

'Not Sharon,' said Carol. 'She'll be all right.'

'You reckon everything's always all right,' said Annie, as though it was a mortal sin.

Annie had measured spoonfuls of instant coffee and was waiting for the kettle to boil. Carol turned her gaze once more to the garden. The only splashes of colour to be seen were a bright yellow Frisbee and two mauve and gold BMX bikes in what had once been a flowerbed. You needed to be an optimist to keep going in this place, and Carol had made her mind up, years ago, that she would keep going.

The kettle boiled. Annie filled the cups, added a sugar bowl and a pathetic plate of biscuits to the tray, and held the kitchen door open for Carol.

Carol clattered down the corridor, successfully negotiated two fire doors by kicking them open and racing through before they had time to swing back on her. She reached the door of the staff sitting room, where the meeting was being held. She held the tray with one hand, and knocked with the other.

The door was opened for her.

As she handed the coffee round, she looked at each adult. There was only one she recognised: Ruth, Sharon's social worker, the only regular caller Sharon had.

Ruth gave her a half smile. The others seemed embarrassed.

Blimey, thought Carol, anyone would think Sharon's dead. And it didn't help, the way they'd all fallen silent.

Only one of the adults spoke to her – a large, breathless woman in hat and coat.

'What's your name, my dear?'

'Carol.'

'Carol. Thank you, Carol. And are they looking after you all right, here?'

Carol looked at Jim. He nodded.

'Yeah,' said Carol. 'How about your kids? All right? Got everything they want?'

The woman flushed.

None of the others said a word. They grabbed their

coffee and a handful of crumbs, and stirred briskly about in their cups, as if glad to have something to do.

Carol wasn't sorry to get back to Annie.

'What about the police?' Annie was rolling out pastry.

'Scotland Yard's baffled,' said Carol.

'Mr Flaskett would tell you if he had any news. Tells you everything, doesn't he?'

'He'd better,' said Carol. 'Place would fall apart if I wasn't kept informed.' She smiled. She was a strong-looking girl with an energy that Jim often found exhausting.

'Did she take much with her?'

'Nothing. Left all her belongings – clothes, toothbrush, everything. Just went in what she was wearing.'

'Middle of the night? Must have been cold. I hope she had a coat.'

Carol looked at Annie, wondering if she was being sarcastic. It didn't seem so. But there was no coat mentioned in Jim's description given to the police: faded blue jeans, a yellow T-shirt, dark brown zip-up 'bomber' jacket and trainers. These were Sharon's favourite old clothes that she put on every day, the minute she got back from school.

'She took her teddy-bear with her,' said Carol.

Annie stopped rolling her pastry and looked at her. They both recognised the significance of this. Sharon had run off before, more than once, but only for a few hours, and only in temper. Carol knew that feeling. You flew out, wanting to scream and shout, and smash something. You went storming down to the shops, or the park, and then, later, when you felt better, you came back or let yourself be found.

But you didn't take your teddy-bear with you.
'And she took money.'
'How much?' asked Annie.
'Thirty quid.'
'Where'd she get that from?'
'Jim's office,' said Carol. 'It was our pocket money.'
'She must have been planning to go a long way.'
Carol doubted it. Sharon didn't make plans.
'She hasn't got any family?'
'No,' said Carol. 'Her mum's dead – died years ago, when Sharon was little. And she's never said anything about her dad.'
'No uncles or aunts?'
'No.'
'Perhaps it's something at school.'
'Doubt it.'
'You can give me a hand with the potatoes,' said Annie, passing Carol a knife.

The meeting was breaking up. They could hear voices in the hall, and the front door being opened.

Jim came into the kitchen. Ruth, Sharon's social worker, was still with him.

'Thanks for the coffee, Annie,' said Jim.
'Did it help?'
'A bit.'
'Who was that nosey old cow who asked me if I was all right?'
'That wasn't a nosey old cow, Carol,' said Jim. 'That was Mrs Bathurst. She's an important person . . .'
'She reckons,' said Carol, quickly.
'. . . and we like to try to keep on the right side of her.'

'She the one that's going to shut this place down?'

'Who said anything about shutting this place down?' Now Jim spoke quickly.

'Sharon.'

'Yes, well – she doesn't own The Laurels, does she?'

Carol shrugged her shoulders. She didn't like it when Jim got that edge to his voice.

Ruth was anxious to go. 'You'll let me know if anything turns up? If you hear anything?'

'Of course,' said Jim.

Ruth moved her briefcase from one hand to the other.

'Do you think Sharon will come back?' she said.

'It's never easy to know what Sharon will do.'

'There was one thing,' said Ruth. 'I checked Sharon's papers yesterday. There are some notes about an uncle she'd once run away from. Not a real uncle. A kind of foster uncle that she used to spend weekends with – that sort of thing.'

'Any idea where he lived?'

Ruth shook her head.

There was a moment's silence.

'You going to peel that potato, or just look at it all day?' said Annie.

Carol threw the potato into the corner of the room.

'Peel your own potato!' she said, angrily.

Jim sighed.

Chapter Five

The three children lay on the floor of the railway coach for several minutes, gulping to get their breath back. Joanne looked across at the girl. Her thin body was heaving, but her eyes were bright with excitement – more than that, a kind of bravado.

''S good that,' said the girl. 'Gave that old wally a run for 'is money.'

'Was his name Wally?' asked Ben. 'Is he a friend of yours?'

The girl grinned.

'Why did he chase us?' said Joanne.

'Must 'ave bin your loony brother 'e was after.'

'No, really, why *did* he chase us. We weren't doing any harm. We weren't even trespassing.'

'Look, 'e ain't from the Council. There's somethin' bent goin' on at that barn place, an' they don't want no one 'angin' about there.'

'Supposing he'd caught us.'

'I'd be ready for 'im,' said the girl.

She pulled up the bottom of her jeans, reached inside the sock, and drew out a knife in a leather sheath. She whipped off the sheath and pointed the knife at Joanne.

Joanne felt her eyes bulge. She glanced at Ben to see if he was frightened. He hadn't even noticed.

'I want something to eat,' he said.
'You got worms?' said the girl.
'I haven't got *anything*,' said Ben.
'Not worms to eat, loony,' said the girl. 'Though I could probably find you the odd earwig, if you're desperate.'
Ben pulled a face.
''E's goin' to be sick,' said the girl. 'You can see.'
'Sick with hunger,' said Ben.
'There's chocolate biscuits in that bottom cupboard. Behind you.'
Ben opened the cupboard and rummaged inside.
The girl replaced the knife in its sheath, and stuck the sheath back in her sock.
'Want a biscuit, Jo?'
Joanne said nothing, but shook her head. The knife still worried her.
'Got anything to drink?' asked Ben.
'Coke.' The girl looked at Joanne. 'Your loony brother got a name?'
'Ben.'
'Nice name for a loony,' said the girl. 'I'm Sharon.'
There was a pause.
''E called you "Jo",' said the girl.
'Yes.'
'Right chatterbox you are. So it's Jo and Ben?'
'Do you live here?' said Ben. 'Is this your house?'
'Ain't mine. But I live 'ere. I'm on the run. Bunked it.'
'From prison?' Ben was almost as interested in this possibility as he was in the chocolate biscuits.
'Course not! Prison! You got a thing about prison.'

'No,' said Ben. 'But that's where they put trouble makers.'

'Thanks a lot,' said Sharon. 'But they don't put twelve-year-olds in prison, do they?'

'Where then?'

'You gonna tell? You gonna tell your mum and dad about me?'

Joanne didn't answer. She looked around. Here she was, sitting on the floor of an old railway coach, littered with unhygienic bits of old food – bread crusts, apple cores, yoghurt pots, drink cans. Mum would have a fit if she saw it. This cramped, grubby little room. Everything greasy, dirty, uncared for.

It was Ben who spoke. 'Where have you run away from?'

'Children's 'ome.'

'Whereabouts?'

'London. Winterbourne Park. Place called The Laurels.'

'Winterbourne Park's near us.'

At last Joanne spoke. 'But why have you run away?'

'You ever bin in a kids' 'ome? No? Well, you wouldn't understand, then.'

The girl sounded unfriendly. It was time to go. Joanne got up to leave. The girl seemed to read her actions like a book.

'Stay to dinner,' she said. 'I got plenty. Sardines, mushy peas, chocolate spread. You can 'ave what you like.'

'We ought to get back to the caravan.'

'Not yet,' said Ben. 'It's only a quarter to twelve. I'm hungry.'

Sharon opened a drawer and took from it a handful of dirty cutlery – knives, forks, spoons. She sorted through them, and found what she was looking for.

'Tin-op'ner. Now, anything you like.'

She and Ben were smiling at each other. Joanne wasn't so sure. She didn't wish Sharon any harm. It must be horrible in a children's home. The play acting of yesterday had been immature and unrealistic. Who'd really want to be an orphan? All right – she wouldn't tell on Sharon, not unless someone asked directly about her. But it didn't seem a good idea for her and Ben to get mixed up in this business.

'We ought to go home,' Joanne repeated.

Sharon was holding out her hands towards Joanne. In one hand was a tin of beans, in the other a tin-opener. It was as though the tough girl was pleading.

Ben had already plunged his finger into a jar of chocolate spread. In between mouthfuls, he said: 'Let's stay, Jo, it's like a real adventure.'

Was that what they were being offered? Not just cold baked beans, but adventure? Well, it would certainly be something to tell the others back at school.

'Well,' said Joanne, as if she was at some polite party, 'if you're really sure you can spare some beans . . .'

'Bit posh, aren't you?'

They ate the beans, and then a tin of pears and a tin of evaporated milk. Sharon's entire larder consisted of tins, jars and packets. There was no fresh food, and nothing that needed cooking or preparation.

While they ate, Sharon explained.

'Got no cooker. Disconnected. An' anyway, if I

cooked anythin' it would mean saucepans an' washin' up. No 'ot water. An' I like eatin' out a tin.'

'But what's going to happen when the people who live here come back?'

'Nobody lives 'ere. It's jus' an old shack by the sea. Who's gonna come down 'ere? I bin down this way before. Yonks ago. There was no one livin' in it then, and there's no one livin' in it now.'

'But what about The Laurels?'

'Stuff The Laurels. They don't know about this place. They ain't gonna look 'ere.'

'What about the police, then?'

'It's a big place, England. But I do 'ave to keep a bit out of the way. Place like this, they notice strangers. It's all right in 'oliday time, but not now. That's where you come in. That's why I chose you.'

'Chose us? What for?' The uneasy feeling returned to Joanne. This girl was always far too many jumps ahead.

''Ow often d'you come down to that caravan of yours? Ev'ry weekend?'

'We've only just bought it,' said Ben. 'This is our first visit.'

'Your dad expectin' a lot of rain?'

'What?'

'Buildin' Noah's Ark, ain't he? Never seen so much wood go in anywhere. Thought you must be buildin' a boat, emigratin'. Goin' back to Jamaica.'

'We live in Forest Hill,' said Joanne.

'I know Forest Hill. That's only a couple of miles from The Laurels. See – I was right to choose you.'

'But what have you chosen us for?'

'Do my shoppin'. So I can keep out of sight. So the police don't come into it.'

'We can't. We won't be here. Not for weeks. Maybe not till spring.'

Sharon looked troubled. 'You got to. I chose you. I can't manage alone.'

'But it isn't up to us. We don't decide,' said Joanne. 'Our parents do.'

'So what?'

'They're bigger than us,' said Ben.

'What's so big about them!' said Sharon, scornfully. 'At The Laurels we 'ad 'undreds of bleedin' adults. Shifts of 'em!'

'It's not like that with Mum and Dad.'

'Why?'

It was too hard to explain. Mum and Dad didn't come on duty. They were there all the time. Like now – they'd be waiting. You had to keep to the family timetable, the family rules.

'We must go,' said Joanne. 'Honestly. We said we'd be back.'

'What about this afternoon?'

'I feel sick,' said Ben.

'Shut up about being sick,' said Sharon, angrily. 'What about my shoppin'?'

'Why can't you do it?'

Sharon sneered. 'Because I got to stay out of sight.'

'Is that why we had to run away from Mr Wally?'

'You go and be sick, loony,' said Sharon. She turned to Joanne. 'Look – I got money. I got a list. You go to that shop on the caravan site and buy enough to tide me over. Then get your mum and dad to bring you back 'ere in a couple of weeks. I got to 'ave food.'

Sharon produced a crumpled piece of paper from her pocket and flapped it at Joanne.

'Do it. We could be mates. 'Ave a good bit of fun. Find out about that barn place, an' that wally on the motor-bike.'

'Yes,' said Ben. 'I'd like to. Because it doesn't make sense.'

'That's it,' said Sharon, eagerly. 'Dogs on the tape – barmy.'

'It's not that,' said Ben. 'There's something else. Did you see what he put in the pannier of his bike? Before he chased us?'

'No,' said Joanne.

'It was a football.'

Chapter Six

Lunch in the caravan was awful.

'Come on, Ben,' said Dad, cheerily. 'Eat up!'

'And you, Jo, all that fresh air must have given you an appetite.'

'Sausages and beans! Your favourite!'

'What? Oh, yes.' Ben forced a ghastly smile to his face, and placed one baked bean on his fork. 'Yum, yum,' he said, in a voice of despair.

'You don't have to be so polite, Ben,' said Mum. 'We're not at Granny's. You could put two whole beans in at a time.'

It was lucky their parents were in such a good mood. Dad kept leaping up from the table to run his hands proudly along the edge of a new shelf unit. Mum was washing up and looking forward to going home.

'Hot water out of a tap, and a proper sink with a waste-pipe. Not a bucket under the floor.'

While her parents' backs were turned, Joanne quickly dropped one of her sausages on to Ben's plate.

'Hey, that's not fair . . .'

A smart kick under the table silenced him.

Mum spun round. 'I hope you're not trying to pinch Ben's food?'

'Heavens, no,' Joanne smiled sweetly.

'And what are you two doing this afternoon?'

Joanne had been waiting for this question. It was not often she told her father or mother a direct lie, but she'd seen this one coming a mile off. The worry was, would one lie lead to another, and another?

'Ben wants to go for a walk. Don't you, Ben?'

'No, I . . .'

One kick led to another kick.

'Ouch! Yes, I . . .'

'He wants to fly his kite.'

'Do I? Yes. Ouch! Yes. Yes, yes, yes. I do.'

'Stop wriggling about, Ben,' said Mum. 'Anyone would think you'd got worms.'

'How did you know about me and worms?' Ben was genuinely amazed.

It was time to get out of the caravan. Before Ben put his foot right in it. Before Mum plonked some great big pudding on the table and demanded that they eat it.

In the pocket of her jeans, Joanne could feel Sharon's money and Sharon's shopping list. Highly incriminating evidence. Impossible to explain if they fell out. Leave now, while the going's good. Time for a quick getaway.

'Come on, Ben. Hurry up.'

'You can take your pudding with you,' said Mum. 'It's only fruit.'

They grabbed the bananas from the table.

'Let's go fly the kite,' said Joanne.

'Yes,' said Ben. 'Yes, yes.' And then once more, so that it sounded extremely strange. 'Yes.'

'Have you been drinking?' asked Mum.

'Yes,' said Ben. 'Coke. How did you know?'

Joanne groaned.

'I didn't mean Coke. I meant alcohol. You seem so strange. And you're not supposed to buy Coke!'

'I didn't . . .'

Ben broke off, realising the mistake he was about to make.

'Tea'll be at six.'

'Please, I don't want any tea,' said Ben.

'Of course you do. I'll make a pile of sandwiches. I'm not going back to The Stores to do any more shopping this holiday.'

Joanne looked quickly at Ben.

'We can have a proper meal when we get home. Don't be late.'

The children leapt for the door, Ben snatching up his kite as he did so. They jumped down from the caravan on to the grass and started to race away.

'Just a minute!' It was Mum, calling from the doorway.

Had she discovered something? Both children froze, almost in mid-stride. Joanne had to force herself to turn round.

'Ben!'

'Yes?'

'Turn round.'

'Can't.'

'Why not?'

'Er, stiff neck.'

'Worms, no appetite, stiff neck. Perhaps you ought to go to hospital.'

Joanne couldn't bear the suspense. 'What did you want, Mum?'

'I wanted to know what to do with his smelly junk.'

'Chuck it away,' Ben called back.
'Now I know you're sick.'
The children heard the caravan door slam shut.
'Thank goodness. Come on, before Mum thinks of something else.'
Mum's expertise never failed to astonish Ben.
'How did she know I feel sick?' he said.
Joanne led him hurriedly away, through the gap in the blackberry bushes, and out of the caravan park by what they called the 'back door', into Dog's Hill Lane.
As soon as they were safely out of sight, Ben slowed down and began to complain.
'Why this way? I thought we were supposed to be doing Sharon's shopping.'
'We are.' Joanne urged him on past the bungalows of the Ridgeway. 'But we've got to approach The Stores from the other side. By the church. If we go the usual way, Mum and Dad may see us.'
'It's a wonder I can approach at all,' said Ben. 'Stones, kicks. Crippled for life. Ought to get compensation.'
'Rubbish,' said Joanne.
'Ought to be allowed to go the short way, then.'
'This way's safe.'
They reached the footpath that led to the church, and a few minutes later were back on the main road.
'You wait here,' said Joanne, 'and I'll do the first lot of shopping. Don't talk to anyone. And act natural!'
A very puzzled Ben waited at the church, while Joanne hurried to The Stores.
Act natural!
Ben had never felt so unnatural in his life. The minutes

dragged by. He frequently consulted his digital watch. Two ten . . . thirteen . . . fifteen . . . sixteen . . . A few cars passed. A couple of bikes. The occasional coach. Everyone seemed to stare at him.

At two thirty-six, Joanne staggered back with a large cardboard box.

'It was awful,' she said. 'Let's get out of here.'

They carried the box back along the footpath, turned left at the Ridgeway, and set off for the shack.

As they trudged along, Joanne wondered how best to deliver the supplies. They could hardly go up to the front door, the shack was supposed to be empty. Anyone seeing them deliver tinned peaches and packets of cornflakes to an empty house would become curious. The whole thing was getting more complicated by the minute. Suppose the police were waiting at the shack. There'd be dreadful trouble.

Or suppose the owners of the shack had come back unexpectedly? It was all very well for Sharon to say they'd gone away and wouldn't be back.

And there was that knife of Sharon's. A lot of the time Joanne thought about that knife.

'This weighs a ton,' said Ben.

'We're nearly there.'

Joanne said nothing to him about her worries. It was her responsibility, but it bothered her that what had started out as a bit of fun had become so involved.

The problem of how to deliver the groceries was one quickly solved. Sharon met them on the edge of the wood.

'Not the front way,' she said. 'Round the back. This all you got?'

'I couldn't carry all you wanted. And if I'd bought too much the woman at The Stores would have suspected. I had to pretend these were things Mum wanted for tea.'

'That's OK,' said Sharon. 'Ben can get the rest.'

'Not likely,' said Ben.

Half an hour later, a furious Ben was scuffling along the Ridgeway. He had money and bits of shopping list. He had attempted to show his independence by tearing up Sharon's list and throwing the bits on the floor.

They'd made him pick it up. They'd shoved the cardboard box in his hands, the money in his pocket, instructions in his ear.

'Mind what you say.'

'If you wanna nick anything, do it the minute you get in the shop – once you've bin 'angin' about, that's when people start to get suspicious.'

'Don't buy any of the things I've crossed out.'

Ben's only reply had been: 'All right, all right!'

But it wasn't all right.

Shopping! He loathed it.

His face set in a murderous glower, Ben arrived at The Stores.

Stupid shop! Full of things he didn't want. Hot-water bottles, aspirins, sun-hats, newspapers.

He hunted up and down the shelves, filling a trolley with tins of spaghetti, jars of jam, Marmite, cheese spread, packets of crisps. As he found each item, he let a piece of shopping list drop to the floor.

The owner of The Stores followed him round, picking up the pieces. It was like a paperchase.

Ben arrived at the check-out. The girl on the till was local, part-time, and slow.

The Shack by the Sea   47

The owner liked to take a personal interest in her customers. It was good for trade. She stopped to have a chat with Ben.

'Hallo, Ben,' she said.

Ben clutched his trolley for support.

'No,' he said.

'It is Ben, isn't it?'

'Not necessarily,' he said.

'Doing the shopping for Mum?'

'No.' Ben tried to recall the deceit he was practising. Was he shopping for Mum? Or wasn't he? He decided to play safe.

'Might be,' he said.

Why didn't the old faggot mind her own business. That was precisely what the old faggot was doing.

'Going home today?' she asked.

'Yes.' She wasn't going to catch him out again!

'Are you sure your mother wants all this?'

'Yes.'

'Your sister bought a lot of things earlier.'

'Yes.'

The faggot looked at the tins. 'Spaghetti *and* macaroni,' she said. 'And which do you like best?'

'Yes.' It occurred to Ben that this wasn't a very good answer.

'All these Mars bars,' said the faggot. 'You'll be sick!'

'They're not for me,' said Ben, hurriedly. 'They're for Shar . . . sharing. For sharing.' Why didn't the girl on the till get a move on!

'It looks like you're going to have a party,' said the faggot.

'Yes,' said Ben, miserably. Inspiration came. 'It's a wedding. My aunt's marrying one of my uncles.'

'Today?'

There wouldn't be time, thought Ben, with deep cunning. 'Tomorrow,' he said. 'Early. Eight o'clock.' He felt quite smug.

'Sunday? That's not normal! Are they some special religion?'

'Yes.'

Wilder still and wilder, Ben's thoughts roamed. He tried to recall any relevant fact about his uncle and aunt. They lived in Yorkshire – Bradford. A phrase came to mind.

'They're with the Bradford and Dingley,' he said.

The faggot smiled politely, wondering what on earth he was talking about.

At last the girl on the till was ready for him. Ben began to unload his trolley.

At this moment there was a squeal of brakes from the car park outside The Stores. A car door slammed. The shop door was flung open, and a man strolled in. He was tall, dressed in a blue denim shirt and jeans. He wore dark glasses and was smoking a long cigarette.

Ben watched out of the corner of his eye, as the man walked to the side of the shop where beach balls, buckets, and other toys were stacked. The man grabbed four plastic footballs, cradled them in his long arms, and joined the queue behind Ben.

The faggot was quickly into conversation.

'Well,' she said to the man, 'you must have a big family.'

The man spoke without removing the cigarette from his mouth.

'Yeah, kids.'

Ben's cardboard box of groceries was ready.

'Ten twenty-eight,' said the girl on the till.

'No,' said Ben, worried about the time. 'Three fifty-six.' He pointed to his watch.

'Ten *pounds* twenty-eight,' said the girl. She pointed to the till.

Ben, feeling foolish and cross, fished the money from his pocket, waited for the change, picked up his box, and staggered to the door.

As he did so, he saw the man in dark glasses paying for the footballs with a fifty-pound note.

Flash, thought Ben.

The man was clearly in a hurry. He was in his car before Ben had crossed the car park, and forced Ben into the hedge as he drove out, tyres whirring on the gravel. There was enough aggression in his hurry to frighten Ben.

'Evil,' said Ben, half aloud. 'Dark glasses like that. Fag in his mouth. Evil.'

It was a bright afternoon for late October. Bright enough for the vicar of St Richard's Church to be wearing his dark glasses as he came out of his church, just as Ben reached the corner.

'There's another one,' said Ben. 'Evil.'

The vicar smiled, as he always did when he didn't hear what people said to him.

Chapter Seven

At The Laurels, Carol walked briskly along the corridor to Sharon's bedroom. Looked? They *said* they'd looked, but they wouldn't know where to look! Never mind a needle in a haystack, Carol reckoned Jim wouldn't be able to find the haystack.

Never mind. She'd do it.

She ignored the notice on the door of Sharon's room.

PRIVAT
KEEP YORSELF OUT
THAT MEANS *YOU*!!!

It was time people stopped fussing about rules and regulations, and got down to finding Sharon. If the police couldn't do it, and Ruth couldn't do it, and Jim couldn't do it – well, it was obvious, she'd have to.

The room was tidy. Not Sharon's doing. Normally it was like a tip. Pop posters on the walls, and a swimming certificate – 'Bronze Award for Personal Survival'. Sharon had pinched it from another kid at school.

There was a small bedside cabinet, a chest-of-drawers, and a wardrobe.

Start with the cabinet.

Nothing.

The wardrobe.

Clothes, shoes, and a fruity smell.

Not for a moment did Carol lose confidence. Nothing in the cabinet and the wardrobe? Then there'd be something in the chest-of-drawers.

It was her rule never to do things by half. If you pulled a drawer out, then you pulled it right out, and put it on the floor. That way, you could search properly.

Start with the top drawer.

Junk. Make-up. Boxes. Bits of plastic. And what Sharon called her 'jewels'.

Middle drawer. Tights, leg-warmers, underwear.

Bottom drawer. Sweaters, and Sharon's grubby track-suit.

Nothing.

Carol was disappointed. She shoved the last drawer back into its place. It wouldn't close properly. Something was jamming it, stopping it sliding all the way home.

Carol yanked the drawer out again, knelt on the floor and squinted into the chest. She couldn't see anything, so she reached in with her arm, and ran her hand along the back panel.

Wedged in the corner was an envelope.

Aha!

Carol sat on the bed and examined what she'd found.

It was addressed to Sharon. At Rowandale. Where she'd lived before they'd sent her to The Laurels. Posted four years ago in south-east London. It was tatty and dog-eared. Not like something you looked at once and never again. Important.

Jim had a very strict rule – nobody opened other people's letters.

Very sweet, very touching.

Carol had a different rule – always poke your nose in. She pushed back the flap and drew out the contents.

A photograph. Also creased. A colour photo and not a good one. Probably taken with an instant camera. A photo of a man with white hair and a beard, and a young girl – Sharon, aged about eight. Carol had no idea who the man was. The two were sitting on the cabin of a small boat, leaning against the mast. The old man was smiling. Sharon was pulling a face.

Carol turned the photo over. On the back was a simple message: 'Love from Neddie'.

What a name! Neddie! Never heard that one before! Sharon had never said a word about him, the secretive little so-and-so.

There were no other clues. The photo could have been taken anywhere. Wooden pilings, a jetty, flat land. No buildings, so it couldn't have been London.

Well, time for action. Time to get Jim going. Time he started finding Sharon.

Carol was determined that he should.

She bustled back along the corridor, down the stairs, and into Jim's office.

He was sitting at his desk, a folder open in front of him, a piece of paper in his hands. He smiled, wearily, as Carol breezed in.

'Here you are, Sherlock,' she said, handing him the photo. 'Clue for you. Get the violin warmed up and put your dressing-gown on.'

Jim stared at the photo.

'Sharon,' he said.

Carol snapped her fingers. 'You're so *quick*,' she said.

Jim ignored her merry sarcasm.

'And who's this with her?'

'Neddie.'

Jim raised his eyebrows.

'You don't believe me?' said Carol. 'Look on the back.'

Jim looked. She handed him the envelope.

'Well – come on, Sherlock. What are you going to do?'

'No idea,' he said. 'They look happy enough. A river – a small cruiser. A bit like a fishing-boat. Red, with a white cabin and a varnished wooden mast.'

'There you go again!' said Carol. 'I dunno how you do it.'

'Elementary, my dear . . . er . . . er . . .'

'Carol,' said Carol.

'Of course,' said Jim. 'The point is – where was the photo taken? How's your geography, Carol?'

Carol smiled sweetly. 'I do office practice instead,' she said.

'Fine,' said Jim. 'You tidy my desk while I have a think. It could be East Anglia. The Broads. It could be the Isle of Sheppey.' He reached for the telephone. 'I'll call Ruth.'

When Ruth answered the phone, Jim said: 'I've found a photo . . .'

'Old liar,' muttered Carol.

Jim pulled a face.

'. . . my glamorous assistant has found a photo. Taken a few years ago. It's of Sharon and a man. Fairly old. On a boat somewhere. On the back it says "Love from Neddie". So – who's Neddie?'

Carol could hear only Jim's side of the conversation.

'Might be,' he said. 'Can you try? Good . . . yes . . . How about Rowandale?'

Carol sensed his spirits lifting, slightly.

'. . . right, Ruth . . . Thanks a lot. 'Bye.'

Jim replaced the phone.

'All sorted out?' said Carol.

'Ruth thinks Neddie might be the uncle who used to take Sharon out. She's going to try to trace him. It's a chance.'

The phone rang.

'That was quick,' said Carol.

Jim gave her a sardonic smile as he answered the phone. Then he frowned, the smile disappeared, and the weary look returned.

'Hallo, Mrs Bathurst,' he said. He cupped his hand over the mouthpiece. 'I think you'd better scram, Watson. Do you mind?'

'It's the old cow,' said Carol. 'You tell her – she's got nothing to worry about. Sharon's as good as found.'

But Jim was already concentrating deeply. He waved Carol out, and, taking the hint, she got up and left.

'We'll find her,' she said, over her shoulder. 'You tell the old cow. We'll find her.'

Chapter Eight

The carriage floor was flush with the ground. Already the process by which it would rot and crumble to pieces was well advanced. It was under attack by weather and weevil. Attempts had been made at either end of the shack to prolong its life by nailing on outer clapboard walls, and a tarpaulin roof had been fastened over the top, extending on one side to form a verandah.

Inside, the bulkheads had been removed to provide a living-room, a bedroom and a kitchen. There was no lavatory. The fittings in all three rooms were broken and useless. The furniture, such as remained, was damp, mouldy and falling to pieces. There was no doubt that the shack was derelict and abandoned.

At one time it must have been lived in, but the closer Joanne looked, the more she realised that Sharon was right not to fear the return of the owners. The brown and cream paint was peeling from its walls, littering the floor like giant dandruff. The windows were all stuck fast, so that it was impossible to open them.

There was also very little doubt in Joanne's mind, that it would be quite impossible for Sharon to survive here much longer. A few days, a couple of weeks at the most. Gales would soon lash up the Channel, pounding the East Sussex coast. Joanne looked around her. There was no sign of heating. Tomorrow the clocks would go back. It would be dark very early. The nights would get longer and longer. She shuddered when she imagined Sharon – cold, wet, and utterly alone in the darkness.

''S good, innit,' said Sharon.

'Yes.' It seemed impossible to say otherwise.

'Bet you wish you 'ad a place like this – all yours.'

'Yes.'

'Place you could do up, jus' 'ow you liked.'

Joanne looked again at the walls. The damp had risen to waist level.

'Yes,' she said.

'Sort out the furniture.'

The cracking, wrinkled, disintegrating furniture.

'Make it all really nice.'

Joanne's discomfort increased. Sharon imagined something out of 'Homes and Gardens'. Joanne imagined something out of 'Hammer House of Horror'. Any night Sharon spent here could be so dangerous. An old tramp could barge in. Or the shack could catch fire. Didn't Sharon care about things like that?

The sensible thing would be for Joanne to tell her parents. Or perhaps an anonymous 'phone-call to the police, from one of the call-boxes by The Stores. Just dial 999.

'You ain't gonna grass me up?'

It was as if Sharon could read her thoughts. But it wasn't a question of grassing. It was being in the horrible position of having to decide whether to let Sharon have a bit more time, or bring the wholly silly, dangerous game to a halt.

Ben arrived, hot and cross, with the groceries.

'Probably sprained both my wrists,' he said, looking accusingly at Joanne. 'Hurt my leg. And done something to my stomach, I shouldn't wonder.'

'I'll do something to your ear'ole, in a minute,' said Sharon. 'Did you get everything?'

'Yes, I did.' No amount of threats was going to make him do as he was told this time. 'And that woman at The Stores shoved her nose in. And there was this evil man with dark glasses. Evil, tall, and with deadly shades. Wanted to kill me.'

'Know the feeling,' said Sharon. She was sorting through the box. 'What about the change?'

'Here's the rotten change,' said Ben, handing it over. 'And he bought four footballs.'

'What is it you two 'ave got about footballs?'

'The man from the barns. The man on the motor-bike. The one that chased us. He had a football.'

'So?'

'Yesterday we saw this man on Camber Sands. He threw this football into the sea. Deliberately. Just chucked the football into the sea. Daft.'

Sharon was more interested. 'Same man?'

'Don't know. Couldn't see him clearly. He was too far away.'

''S gotta be somethin' goin' on. What does a wally, or even two wallies, want with a load of footballs? I mean, I know wallies are barmy about football, but it don't make sense. There's somethin' goin' on. Out at them barns.'

Inwardly, Joanne agreed. There probably was something going on, but, compared with the problem of what to do about Sharon and the shack, it didn't seem of the first importance. The barn was 'some*thing*' that was happening over there. Sharon was 'some*body*' that was happening right here.

''Ow about,' Sharon's eyes were gleaming with enthusiasm, 'goin' over to the barns? Won't be anyone there now. 'E's done the batt'ries.'

'What's the time, Ben?' asked Joanne.

'Half past four.'

'We've got to go,' said Joanne. 'Mum told us to be back at five.' She even made it sound like a lie.

Ben opened his mouth, but said nothing.

'Scared,' sneered Sharon.

'No. But we've got to get back. Help clear up. Then we go home.'

'What am I supposed to do! Stay 'ere by meself? Bloody great, that'll be!'

Joanne wanted to leave. 'Look,' she said, 'we'll do what we can. Maybe we can come down soon.'

'Next weekend,' said Sharon, firmly.

'I don't know.'

'Gimme your address in London.' It was an order.

'Why?' For one dreadful moment, Joanne had a vision of Sharon arriving on their doorstep.

'So I can write to you.'

'What's the point? There's no way we can write back.'

''Cos I want someone to write to – that's the point. I can't write to my social worker, can I? Or my teachers, or The Laurels. One look at the postmark an' they'll all be 'ere.'

'No.' Joanne was firm. Going home was the only way to put an end to all this. Go home, without leaving their address, and not come back for weeks. By that time

Sharon would be gone. The police would have found her. In a few hours she and Ben would be home, and then they wouldn't have to make any more decisions.

'All right,' Sharon said. 'We'll sort it out tomorrow.'

'We won't be here tomorrow.'

Sharon smiled. 'We'll sort it out then.'

There was no point in arguing. Joanne opened the door.

'Come on, Ben,' she said.

'See you tomorrow,' said Sharon. 'An' then we'll 'ave another look at the barns an' the dogs.'

Ben followed his sister out of the shack and into the bushes. Joanne looked back. Sharon was leaning in the doorway, staring at them. It was not a friendly stare.

'I thought we were going home tonight,' said Ben.

'We are.'

Joanne hurried him away.

Chapter Nine

Joanne sat in the caravan, elbows on the table, chin on her fists. Everything was packed. Even Dad's clutter of wood-shavings and tools and glue and nails had been packed away. The car was loaded. Another half-hour, three-quarters at most, and the family would be on their way home. Back to Forest Hill. Back to school. Back to normal.

That was if they did leave the caravan tonight.

If?

No, it was when.

It was all very well Sharon saying they'd meet tomorrow. Sharon was a silly little girl. Any time now the police would find her, and she'd get it in the neck, and serve her right.

'You look tired,' said Mum. 'Had a busy day?'

'Sort of.'

'I should say we have,' said Ben, and then he leapt sideways.

'What on earth are you doing?'

'I . . . er . . . I just thought Joanne might kick me. She does, you know.'

'Don't be silly, Ben. That was when you were both younger.'

'Like this morning,' said Ben, sarcastically.

Dad was beaming. He kept stroking a small shelf he had fixed above the cooker.

'Fits absolutely right,' he said. He seemed to be hoping for applause.

'Wonderful,' said Mum. 'We must think of something to put on it. Now, wash your hands and come and sit down. Ben, start eating.'

'Must I?'

'You're not sickening, are you?' said Mum.

'Most of the time,' said Joanne.

'Why does everyone keep going on about my being sick?'

'As far as I'm concerned,' said Mum, 'you're going back to school on Monday, whatever.'

School.

Joanne found herself almost longing for it.

It was getting dark outside.

'Time for the news.' Dad switched on the radio.

Not much longer, thought Joanne. Twenty minutes – and then it would be all over.

It was all bluff. All lies. This story about running away from a children's home. Rubbish. It was half-term. Sharon was probably on a day trip from London. Lots of kids from London had days out at the seaside. That was it – a pile of old lies. Anyone capable of throwing stones at people could lie like mad.

'. . . and there is still no news of the twelve-year-old girl, Sharon Dunscombe, who has been missing from a children's home in south London since Thursday morning . . .'

Ben stared at Joanne.

'. . . Police have issued the following description . . .'

Joanne felt her stomach turn and her neck lock.

It was real.

It was all real.

Now what? Spill the beans? Bring the whole rotten thing to an end? Or sit here, eating, saying nothing, and keeping her foolish promise?

Ben was still staring, eyes bulging, obviously expecting her to take the initiative. Well, it was obvious, wasn't it? She had to tell Mum and Dad.

'Mum . . .' she began.

Crack!

An explosive crack of glass breaking. From outside the caravan, but very near to it. Where the car was.

'My God!' said Dad.

Ben jumped.

'What on earth . . .' Mum's hand flew to her mouth.

Dad moved quickly to the door, opened it and leapt out. Ben and Joanne scrambled after him.

'Be careful!' That was Mum, calling after them.

The car windscreen was shattered.

Most of the glass held together, but it was as though frozen milk covered it. In the centre was a small hole, and here the glass leaned inwards, towards the driver's seat, where a large flint stone lay. The stone must have been thrown very hard and very deliberately.

'Oi! You! Oi!!' Shouts came from a nearby caravan.

'Come back here!'

People were pointing, and calling to each other.

'Over there! Look! There!'

Joanne looked quickly round the caravan site.

A figure – young, lithe, thin, spiky – was racing across the open space in the middle of the site.

'Stop him!'

A half-hearted pursuit had set off.

'You little devil . . .'

Other, harsher words were hurled.

The little devil darted between rows of caravans, appearing from time to time. Even in good light, it would have been difficult to get a clear view of the little devil.

'What's happened?' Mum was standing at the top of the caravan steps.

Dad pointed to the windscreen. 'That,' he said.

A few people came over.

'Nobody hurt?' said one.

'No, no,' said Dad.

'Senseless. Senseless,' said another. 'Kids today – want a bloody good hiding.'

'You want to get on to the police.' There was plenty of advice to be had.

'They're not going to mend the windscreen,' said Dad.

Ben grabbed Joanne's arm and jerked it. He wanted to whisper something to her. She shook her head.

But she had no doubt that he, too, had recognised the fugitive. The little devil wasn't a 'him'. It was Sharon.

Slowly, the other caravanners moved off, still muttering.

'Ought to be locked up . . . disgraceful . . . getting worse and worse . . . where's the sense in it . . .'

A lot of which, Joanne thought, was true.

Dad looked up at Mum.

'Well, we're not going back tonight,' he said.

'Can't we knock out the broken glass and drive without a windscreen?' Mum wasn't happy about staying.

Neither was Joanne.

'I'm not driving in this weather, at night, without a windscreen.'

'Then I'll drive.'

'Nobody's going to drive. I'll go into Hastings tomorrow and see if I can get a new windscreen fitted.'

'Hastings?'

'There won't be anywhere in Rye.'

They were both angry.

'Finish your tea,' said Dad. 'I'll unpack the blessed car.'

Joanne and Ben followed Mum into the caravan. Joanne whispered quickly to Ben: 'Don't say anything about Sharon.'

Inside, they sat in silence, feeling even less like eating fishpaste sandwiches than before. Mum refilled the kettle. She waited impatiently for it to boil tapping her fingers on the draining-board.

Nobody spoke.

The kettle boiled. Mum made a pot of tea. She went to the door, opened it, and called out.

'I've made some tea.'

'Coming.'

Mum slammed the door.

Joanne and Ben continued nibbling in silence. A few minutes passed.

From outside came the sound of breaking glass.

Mum kicked the sink cupboard. The door came off the hinges.

'And there's something else he can mend,' she said.

The Shack by the Sea 65

Joanne felt guilty. She should have warned her parents that something shocking was likely to happen. But how skilfully Sharon had arranged things. She'd said enough to worry Joanne, but not enough so that she could do anything about it.

The door opened again, and Dad entered. He was carrying a couple of suitcases.

'Good evening,' he said. 'I understand this hotel has rooms to let?'

'I'll give you hotel.'

'I've cleared the glass out,' said Dad. Then he noticed the broken cupboard door. 'More violence?' he said.

'There will be.'

Mum was still angry.

'The important thing is no one's been hurt.'

'I'd like to get my hands on the stupid lout that threw the stone.'

That, thought Joanne, mustn't happen. That must be prevented at all costs. And that put an end to any idea of telling her parents about Sharon.

Ben cleared his throat.

He's going to put on his martyred voice, thought Joanne, with some relief, and put himself in the firing line.

'Did you want to say something, Ben?' she asked, sweetly.

'So I won't go ice-skating tomorrow, then?' said Ben.

They all turned and fired at him.

'All right, all right,' he said, holding up his hands as though trying to ward off the bullets. 'All right. I won't ever ask to go ice-skating again.' He paused, then added: 'I can see tomorrow's going to be a rotten day.'

Joanne no more looked forward to it than Ben did.

Sharon had kept her promise. She had made sure that they would all still be at Rye Bay tomorrow. And her stone had smashed all the family's plans.

Chapter Ten

The worn mud paths glistened in the rain. The paving slabs surrounding the washing and lavatory blocks were dark and cold-looking. The whole morning suggested that living in a caravan by the sea was a mistake. And, as far as Joanne's family was concerned, it was a mistake. They weren't supposed to be here, and it would be well after lunch before they could start for Forest Hill.

Joanne was uneasy. Mum was cross.

Dad had set off for Hastings, to get a replacement windscreen.

Joanne wanted to get out of the way and stay out of the way until lunch-time. Even if it meant taking Ben with her. She suggested that he might like to fly his kite.

'There's plenty of wind this morning.'

'It's raining,' said Mum.

'Not much. Just a bit. We could put our anoraks on.'

They were sitting round the table in the caravan. Outside were few signs of life – one or two people hurrying back from The Stores with the Sunday papers, two boys playing football on the grass.

'You might as well,' said Mum.

Joanne grabbed their anoraks, bustled Ben and his kite from the caravan and led the way through the site.

It was cold as well as wet. There was a deserted feeling, as though all the caravans were empty. The wind was blowing strongly, and in it, the long arms of the bramble bushes were lashing to and fro, like the limbs of demented spiders.

The children climbed the ramp to the concrete promenade, and turned north-east, towards Rye. Joanne had a special reason for going this way. She was angry. Angry enough to seek Sharon. Give her a taste of her own medicine – maybe even bung a stone through one of her windows.

A twelve-year-old!! A second-year! That was the way to look at what had happened. Lynsey, Vanessa, all the others, would laugh at her if they thought she'd backed away from a second-year. Never mind the language, the cockiness, the bravado, the dismissive way Sharon talked about adults. Sharon was only twelve, and Joanne was holding on to that fact.

'Where are we going?' said Ben.

'To sort out Sharon.'

'In the rain?'

'No, inside the police station, where it's warm and dry. What do you think?'

Ben sniffed. 'I think: "I wonder what ill luck will befall me today,"' he said.

'You might get pushed off the sea-wall,' said Joanne, as she hurried him along.

'All right, then. How are we going to sort out Sharon?'

Joanne didn't answer. Her plans weren't that definite.

But she set a cracking pace, the wind swirling and squalling about them. The plastic skin of Ben's kite clattered against its dowelling frame as she rushed him along the wall. From time to time, an extra strong gust of wind, slapping against the kite, sent Ben tottering, almost blowing him on to the shingle below. Joanne snatched his anorak collar, and marched him along.

'How much further?' Ben shouted to make himself heard. He wriggled under Joanne's grip, and had the feeling he'd been placed under arrest.

Joanne took no notice.

They came to the point opposite the crossroads. Joanne looked across to the signpost where the paths joined. Five hundred metres away, a small figure was standing – dark, thin, slight. In the old days, Joanne recalled, felons used to be hanged at crossroads. She remembered reading about 'leaden bodies swaying in the wind', and 'corpses clanking in chains'. The small figure wasn't hanging from the signpost, but there was a doomed air about it.

The figure moved, and began to run along the path towards them.

'What's she want?' Ben snorted, grumpily.

It didn't take Sharon long to reach them. She was still wearing the dirty jeans and T-shirt of yesterday. On top, she had a brown zip-up jacket, very much the worse for wear. Her hair, her jacket, the bottoms of her jeans, and her trainers were all wet. She must have been waiting in the wind and rain for a considerable time.

'All right?' she said, by way of greeting.

'I suppose you think you're clever,' Joanne burst out. 'Smashing our windscreen. Do you know what windscreens cost?'

'No,' said Sharon. 'Do you?'

'Very funny. I hope the police think it's funny when they get you.'

The smile went from Sharon's pink face.

'You got proof then? Eh? Proof? 'Ow d'you know it was me chucked that stone? Could 'ave been anyone. Some 'ooligan from your precious caravan park. There's enough of them.'

'We saw you.'

'That's not proof!'

'We *recognised* you.'

'So what if it was me?'

'You ought to pay for it.'

'All right, then! So, I'll pay for it!'

Sharon unzipped a pocket in her jacket and thrust her hand in. She whisked out a handful of money, which she held out to Joanne.

'Go on! Take it! For your bloody windscreen!'

Joanne didn't move, but stared at the outstretched hand. The fist was half-clenched, with the palm up. She could see how deeply bitten the nails were. In places round them, the skin was ripped and raw. In the glistening pink of Sharon's hand – pink except where the knuckles gleamed white – a five-pound note was becoming limp as the rain fell, and was beginning to droop. Joanne knew it was all the money Sharon had left. It was the money she planned to live off. For as long as she could.

Joanne grabbed Ben's collar once more, and renewed their rapid march along the sea wall.

Sharon came after them.

For a while, all three walked in silence. Out in the bay, the tide was moving in, still far beyond the breakwater, but hurrying over the flat sands. Gulls were driving inland, over a field of winter wheat, making for the gravel pits. In the far distance, beyond the barns, they could see the squat outline of the martello tower at Rye Harbour.

Sharon recovered first from the row.

'Going to fly that kite of yours at last?'

Ben looked from Sharon to his sister, and back. One had him by the collar: one was a knife-wielding Amazon. It seemed best to be polite.

'Yes. Thank you.'

'I'll show you a good place.'

She led them off the sea-wall, and along a path that ran along the edge of the Wildlife Conservancy area, stopping at a point halfway to the martello tower, where the path widened.

'Here,' she said.

Joanne couldn't see any reason for arguing.

Ben's kite was nothing particularly grand. It was a simple diamond shape, with a picture of Superman on it, and two long, flowing plastic tails for stability. In this wind there was none of yesterday's launching problems. The first time Joanne held it above her head and threw it upwards, it soared away, with Ben barely able to pay out the line quickly enough. It tugged and tugged at the stick round which the line was coiled.

'Hold tight!' said Joanne. 'Don't for goodness' sake let go.'

The stick leapt in Ben's hands, in a frenzy to escape, like a trapped fish. He tried to pay out the line slowly and carefully, but the kite would have none of it, and pulled for all it was worth. Ben and Superman were having a tug-of-war.

Higher and higher the kite flew, sometimes swooping down as a rogue current of air caught it, but climbing almost vertically as soon as the main breeze picked it up again. Within seconds it reached a height where they could no longer hear the crackling noise of the fabric as the wind buffeted it. Now, all was quiet, save for the puffing of the wind, and, occasionally, as the wind veered, the barking of dogs. From the barns. A repeated background interruption that touched on Joanne's memories of the wild, weird chase of yesterday.

Another problem.

Visit the barns? Or leave them alone?

But Ben and Sharon were concentrating on the kite. They were in a better mood. Sharon was enjoying herself. In the wind and rain, her hair was plastered to her head, with long dark curls stuck over her forehead. Her eyes were bright. She kept pointing to the kite.

'Look at it! Eh! Look!'

There was no need to be told. The eyes of Joanne and Ben were fixed on the dark diamond, swinging, dipping, lifting, at the end of the taut kite-string.

And then, suddenly, it was away.

Ben gave a yell, and half toppled over as the kite-string flew from him, and he was left, holding the lifeless stick in his hands.

Joanne whirled round.

Sharon was standing, gazing at the kite which was being whisked further and further towards the salt-marshes. In her right hand was the sheath knife. It had needed only one swift downward slash to sever the line. She had caught both Joanne and Ben completely off-guard.

'What have you done!' Joanne gave a wail of anguish, rage and shock.

'You rotten bitch!'

Ben aimed a kick at Sharon. She dodged it easily, but he was wild with anger, and pursued her, lashing out repeatedly. She hopped backwards along the path, always too quick for him, always out of reach. With each frustrated effort at revenge, Ben's fury grew.

'Bitch! Bitch, bitch, bitch!'

He was sobbing with rage, and taking no notice of the knife in Sharon's hand. She made no counter-attack, content merely to keep out of range. Had he kicked her – well, Joanne intervened before it got to that. She caught hold of Ben. At first he struggled, roaring with anger, desperate to hurt Sharon.

Gradually his sobs turned to steadier crying.

'Why the hell did you do that?'

It was inexcusable, inexplicable. One minute they were all enjoying themselves, together. The next, there was poor Ben, with murder in his heart, trying to maim Sharon.

Sharon faced Joanne. There was not the slightest sign of remorse.

'I wanted to see what would 'appen if it was free.'

Joanne gasped at the stupidity of it.

'It would blow away!'

'Think I don't know that! You don't understand. Like the others. All talk. All lovely. All friendly. Friends? You don't even know what it means.'

Ben was still crying. He sat on a bank of soaking grass, looking very young, and very little.

Joanne knelt beside him, and tried to comfort him. But she felt too angry to be much help to Ben. She couldn't do anything about Sharon. No, it would take the police. Sharon was too wild, too mean, too stupid to be dealt with by reason. Force. That was what she needed. To be taught how to treat people. To deal with her violence, destruction, lies, attacks.

Either the police got Sharon, or something much more terrible would happen. Joanne felt she was being pushed more and more towards having to make a decision. That was the worst of it. She experienced a very unwelcome sense of responsibility towards Sharon. Soon – *today* – she would be leaving Sharon to cope on her own in that filthy shack. To face the cold and the wet and the dark.

And the problems of the last twenty-four hours.

Could she leave all those behind? With Sharon?

And Ben lay there, crying – maybe for all three of them.

He certainly didn't cry alone. There was no heaving of the shoulders, but tears mixed with rain on Sharon's cheeks.

'I'm sorry,' she said.

'It's no good being sorry.' Just a whisper from Ben, the echo of a phrase hurled at him, time after time.

'I'll get your kite back,' said Sharon.

Ben looked up. 'How?'

'I'll find it.'

'It went miles,' said Joanne.

'No. It didn't. Not miles. Honest. I saw it come down. I'll show you.'

She was off, running down the path. Joanne and Ben followed, more slowly.

Small patches of grass, tufts of weed and sea-kale grew out of the shingle. It was not a place that held out any promise of comfort on this damp, squally day.

Like a tracking dog, zig-zagging this way and that, Sharon crossed the shingle wastes. She left nothing to chance, working her way steadily to the martello tower.

They reached the tower.

It stood like a desert fort, an outer wall and a central redoubt, both circular. The outer wall had originally been about the height of a two storey house, but in many places the top brickwork had crumbled away. Plants had taken a precarious hold in the crevices. On the inland arc of the circle, ivy covered much of the wall, and here a large bank of stone had been piled, so that it was possible to walk to a height level with the top of the wall. A railing was fixed here, to stop anyone falling into the dried-up moat below.

The children climbed the bank of stones, and looked down into the moat. Among the cans and paper and bits of plastic, they could see Ben's kite, feebly flapping, where it was impaled on a bramble bush.

'Told you I'd find it!' Sharon was triumphant.

'Now you can go and get it,' said Ben.

She didn't hesitate. She selected her point, where the creeper was thick and firm, and swung down. She freed the kite and stood at the bottom of the moat. She looked very small. Like a prisoner.

Sharon pointed up at the tower. It was much higher than the outer wall, and solid enough to withstand any amount of battering. The small windows, high up, revealed just how thick the walls were, for the apertures were thick cut and dark. The tower was in a better state of preservation than the outer wall. Only the ivy gave it any aura of the picturesque, the romantic. In all other ways it appeared a sturdy, utilitarian building.

Sharon was pointing at one of the windows.

'Good job your kite didn't fly in there. Don't fancy 'avin' to climb that wall.'

Joanne wondered how Sharon would get out of the moat. She needn't have worried. Almost as quickly as she had scrambled down the creeper, Sharon clambered up again, carrying the kite in her mouth. She reached the top, panting only a little.

'There,' she said, handing the kite back to Ben.

He took it with no word of thanks.

'We're going home,' said Joanne. 'Come on, Ben.'

''Ang about!' Sharon ran after them, and caught Joanne by the elbow. 'Thought you might like to know. There is a quicker way.'

'Steal a motor-car, I suppose,' said Joanne.

'Ever so witty, aren't we. There's another path, as it happens.'

Joanne looked at Ben's watch. Gone twelve. It was a long way to the caravan. They should get back as quickly as possible. But was it a good idea to accept Sharon's advice?

'All right,' she said.

'How come you know so much about this place?' Ben asked.

After a moment's hesitation, Sharon answered with a shrug of her shoulders.

'I used to come down 'ere. Few times. When I was little. 'Bout your age.' She looked at Ben.

Then she headed along the road that led to Rye. After a couple of hundred metres, she turned left, down a narrow path by the side of a builder's yard. They were soon back in open country, heading towards Winchelsea

Beach. The rain had stopped, and the wind was nothing like as strong as it had been.

The first thing that struck Joanne was that she could hear the dogs again. The barking was steady and continuous, and came from straight ahead. The path they were on went right past the barns. Was this another trick on Sharon's part? Another attempt to inveigle them into her frightening adventures? This time, Joanne promised herself, she'd have an answer ready for Sharon. There'd be no ''Ow about 'avin' a look in'. Joanne knew the way to the caravan well enough from here. This path was the track to the crossroads. There was no need now for Sharon's 'guidance'. She quickened her pace.

''Ere,' said Sharon, 'why don't we . . .'

'No,' said Joanne. 'We're going back to the caravan. You can do what you like.'

Sharon was impressed. 'You catch on, don't you.' There was even a hint of respect in her voice.

At the crossroads, they stopped. Joanne hoped that this would finally be the parting of the ways. But it was not easy to know how to make the goodbyes. Yesterday Sharon had been so sure of herself, so positive that she could keep them here. Today – she was chirpy, but less certain.

'You gonna tell?'

Joanne looked at the ground and shook her head.

'I know it won't last,' said Sharon. 'But not yet. I jus' want a bit more time. They'll get me in the end. But not yet. I can manage. I got food. Roof over me 'ead. Try an' get your mum an' dad to bring you down again soon. An' 'ow 'bout Christmas? We could all meet up Christmas. That'd be a right laugh.'

Joanne nodded.

Christmas! That was weeks and weeks away.

'Your parents open your letters?'

'No.'

'There you are, then. I'll write to you. Give you all the news. What's your address?'

A question – not a command.

From a jacket pocket, Sharon produced a grubby piece of paper and a stump of pencil. Like an eager reporter, she stood there, ready to take down the vital information.

Joanne could not refuse.

'169, Cornwall Road, Forest Hill, London SE23.'

'I'll write,' said Sharon. 'Promise.'

They fell silent.

Ben fidgeted, uncomfortably. 'I'm hungry,' he said, very softly.

'Yeah,' said Sharon. 'Time I got me dinner. See you.'

She had tried to sound cocky. It hadn't worked. She ran over the rise that led to the wood, and was soon out of sight.

'Are you crying?' Ben looked at his sister.

'No,' said Joanne, as she wiped her eye.

'I am.'

'Come on. It's nearly lunch-time.'

None of the children noticed that the barking of the dogs had stopped. The dogs had gone completely from their minds. And none of them thought to look back along the track, towards the barns. If they had, they might have realised that they were being watched. By the man on the motor-bike. They hadn't seen him, but he had certainly seen them, and, for some minutes, had been peering at them most intently, through a pair of powerful binoculars.

Chapter Eleven

Carol went straight to Jim after school on Monday. The tea and buns could wait.

'Any news?'

'Not much. Ruth phoned.'

'You find that Neddie?'

'No – but one of Ruth's colleagues seemed to remember him. Thought he'd been a cab-driver in Plumstead or Woolwich.'

'You ought to be able to find him.'

'I'm trying.'

'Phone the minicab companies.'

Jim smiled patiently. 'I have, Carol,' he said. 'Fifteen of them. None of them have ever heard of a "Neddie". Some of them thought it all very amusing. I've also had Mrs Bathurst breathing fire at me – but I'm not supposed to tell you that.'

Sean, one of the houseparents, put his head round the door.

'They want to know about Sharon,' he said. 'What shall I tell them?'

'Say there's no news. I'll come and join you in a minute. Any trouble?'

'Not really. They all look a bit dopey. Gazing at the telly. But they do want to know about Sharon.'

Sean left.

Jim looked at Carol.

'Be a fight tonight,' said Carol.

'Not tonight, Carol,' said Jim. 'Not tonight, please. I'm on duty.'

'It won't be me,' said Carol. 'I'm talking about the kids. There'll be a fight tonight, betcha. Still, you got one less to bother about, without Sharon.'

'Sharon was never any trouble at night,' said Jim, stung by Carol's sarcasm. 'Slept like a babe. Looked like an angel. It was when she was awake . . .'

'You keep saying "was".'

Jim sighed.

'Let's go and join the others,' he said.

They went through three sets of doors and down the brightly lit corridor, Carol's heels clattering on the floor tiles. In the television room, the children were lolling about on chairs, looking towards the television screen, but not focusing on it, not watching it.

Five o'clock. 'John Craven's Newsround'. Another hour before tea proper. Monday night – shepherd's pie, baked beans, and spaghetti. Filled you up if it didn't do a lot for your skin or figure, thought Carol. Kids' stuff. The whole place was run for kids.

'. . . twelve year old Sharon Dunscombe, who ran away from her children's home in south London . . .'

The children sat up straight, eyes riveted on the screen.

There was a picture of Sharon. Almost unrecognisable, but Carol could identify it as a giant blow-up of the photo of Sharon and Neddie that she had found two nights ago in Sharon's room.

Sharon was out of focus, with very indistinct features.

Some of the younger children didn't believe it was her.

'That ain't Sharon. That kid's too young.'

'It's an old photo,' said Jim, quietly.

They turned to him.

'How d'you know?'

'I gave it to the police.'

'Where d'you get it?'

Carol wondered what he'd say.

'It was found in her room,' said Jim.

There was a slight jeer.

'So you been searching people's rooms!'

'I looked in Sharon's.'

'Why d'you give it to the police?'

'Why d'you think, dopey?'

They were beginning to argue.

'Who's that old geezer with her, Jim?'

'That 'er dad?'

'It's a dirty old man!'

'You shut your face!' said Carol.

'You gonna make me!'

'If I have to!'

Jim stepped in.

'OK, OK,' he said, as calmly as he could. 'Let's settle down. All I hope is that the photo helps us find Sharon. That's the important thing. Maybe this'll do some good.'

They were not going to be easily reassured.

'If they find Sharon, will she go to prison?'

'Don't be stupid!'

'Who you calling "stupid"?'

'Just shut your face.'

'Shut yours.'

Jim stepped in again, to prevent what looked like the start of a fight.

He looked at Carol.

'Told you,' she said. 'Tears before bedtime.'

'Yeah,' said Jim. 'Probably mine.'

Chapter Twelve

Joanne sat at her dressing-table, brushing her hair and gazing at herself in the mirror. Things were getting back to normal. It was Thursday morning – she'd had three whole days at school. Back to a reassuring way of life, where you knew what was what and who was who. No shocks, no surprises, no unbearable responsibilities.

It was nice to brush her hair. And she was beginning to enjoy looking at herself in the mirror.

Life would be very pleasant, if it wasn't for two things. Two people. Ben and Sharon.

She would have to put up with Ben. And he was getting better. Slowly.

Sharon?

Her thoughts kept going back to Sharon.

With that stone in her hand. That knife in her hand. In that grotty shack. All alone, Starving? Freezing? Ill?

Ben had seen 'John Craven's Newsround', and had told his sister all about it. That hadn't helped – to know that police, all over the country, were searching for Sharon, while she, Joanne Lewis, knew exactly where the missing girl was hiding. And could, and *should*, take them straight to her.

She wondered what Sharon was doing at this moment. Not brushing her hair, that was for sure.

Her mother called from downstairs.

'Jo! Letter for you.'

'Coming.'

She hurried down.

Mum was holding the letter in her hand.

'Postmarked Hastings,' she said. 'Some secret admirer?'

'No,' said Joanne. But too hastily.

'Huh,' snorted Ben. 'Anyone who admired you would want to keep it a secret. In case they got locked up as a loony.'

'Have you cleaned your shoes, Ben?'

'Shoes?' Ben's voice implied that he hadn't had anything to do with shoes for some months now.

'Clean them. There's polish and rags under the sink.'

'I know, I know,' grumbled Ben.

Joanne held out her hand for the letter. Her mother handed it to her, but Joanne made no move towards opening it.

'Saving it for later?'

'Er, yes,' said Joanne.

'Secret?'

'Er, private.'

'*Both* shoes, Ben,' said Mum.

'What?'

'Both shoes. You'll be wearing one on each foot, you see. And have either of you seen your father's cheque card?'

'Not since the caravan,' said Ben.

'Yes. That's what he says. Jo?'

'Me?'

Mum stared at her. 'I'm beginning to think they must put some kind of drug in breakfast cereals. Both of you seem particularly slow this morning. Have – you – seen – Dad's – cheque – card?'

'Not since the caravan. Like Ben said.'

Joanne turned quickly away. shoving the letter in her school-bag, and hoping that her mother would leave her alone. She hadn't seen the cheque card since the caravan. But she knew where it was. She'd hidden it. In one of Dad's nice new cupboards in the caravan. There had to be a reason for going back to Winchelsea. It was the best Joanne could think of at such short notice. The whole family had to return. So that she could check up on Sharon.

At least, that was how it had seemed last Sunday.

Meantime, she needed a quick exit.

'I'm off, Mum,' she said. 'See you tonight.'

While she waited for the bus to school, Joanne tore open the letter and read it. The writing was scrawly, hard to read, and the spelling and punctuation didn't help. But the style was friendly, and unmistakably Sharon's.

> Hi Jo
> Hi Ben
> Come on down!!!!!
> And play hunt the Wallies.
> Hurry up – I have been thinking about
> Christmas. You can get Christmas pudings
> in tins. You can get custard in tins.
> We can have a proper Christmas diner in
> the shack.
> Hows about that then!!!!!
> Wot a larf!!!!!

Dont forget
Hurry up – come down this weekend
Its Teusday now only 3 more days and
you will be here.
See you Jo
See you Ben
Wot a larf!!!!!
Sharon.

The bus came. Joanne thrust the letter back in her bag and hoped that maths and double biology would help her forget it.

Chapter Thirteen

Loneliness. Cold nights. Mists in the morning. Damp. And chill, rushing in from the sea and the marshes. More like winter than autumn. Grey skies in the morning. Grey afternoons. And black nights. With everything soaking wet all the time. Three days since she'd spoken to anyone – the woman in the post office: when she bought a stamp for her letter to Joanne.

Sharon was facing the harsh realities of her situation. It had started off fine. Thirty quid in her pocket, and a free train ride to Winchelsea. Go where she liked – do anything she wanted. And she'd paid that lot back in London: Ruth, Jim, the Graingers – serve 'em all right.

But there had been no sign of the sun for a couple of days, and the shack had become cruel cold at nights. She had constructed a makeshift bed from cardboard boxes and some plastic fertiliser sacks she had found at a nearby farm. Didn't match up to the central heating at The Laurels, though, or her bouncy mattress.

She wondered how much longer she could keep going.

Cold and loneliness. And worry about her health. She hadn't bargained for that. What would she do if she became ill? She hadn't been ill for yonks, but that didn't mean anything. Cold, flu, cough – all bad enough. But suppose it was something really serious? There'd be nothing she could do. She might even die. It wasn't a comforting thought.

Money.

The last three days, since Joanne and Ben had deserted her, had shown how quickly she would run out of money. Eight quid left. Still lots of supplies, but cold tinned food was getting on her nerves. Three nights running, she'd been to the cafe at Winchelsea Beach for chicken and chips. It was expensive. It was a risk. But it was worth it for the bright lights and warmth, as much as for the food.

Drink.

That was a problem. She'd made an awful mess here. There was no water at the shack, and the nearest drinking fountain, a mile away, by the caravan park, had been vandalised. She had a couple of Cokes left, but was already fed up with the stuff. What she longed for was water. Run the tap till it was good and cold, and then gulp it down. Glass after glass.

Washing wasn't a problem, there was always the sea. Drying was – she hadn't thought to bring a towel from The Laurels. And she missed her toothbrush. You only got one set of gnashers, didn't you? And they had to last a lifetime. However long that was.

Loneliness and cold and no water.

By Wednesday afternoon she had made up her mind. The only answer to the water problem and the towel problem and the soluble aspirin problem – in case she became ill – was nicking. From now on it was down to nicking for survival. Save all her cash for emergencies.

Caution told her that she ought not to steal from her

own doorstep. But she didn't listen to caution, even when making one of the few plans in her life.

Nicking.

Place: The Stores, they'd got what she wanted.

Time: as soon as possible.

Have to be at night. The dead hour.

Got no watch. Guess – there was no way of telling the time. All she knew was the nights lasted a good deal longer than she expected. Terrifying. She hated the silence, and dreaded any sound. The dead leaves rustling on the trees, and then fluttering to the ground. The hiss of the waves on the shingle as the tide pounded up the beach. Creaking branches. Night noises of birds. Once or twice she thought she heard footsteps. She wondered if soluble aspirin was any good for heart attacks.

By Thursday night she had steeled herself to make a move. Long after it had grown dark she waited, exhausted by worry, hugging Teddy on her makeshift bed.

What time was it now? Surely it was late enough? The dead hour. Felt like it. There wouldn't be anyone about now. Even so, it gave you the willies. As though people hunting her had surrounded the shack. One foot outside and they'd get her!

Rubbish! There was no one there.

With hands that trembled, Sharon fastened her jacket up to the neck and stepped out.

It was a cloudy night, with no moon. The wood was in total darkness, a light wind sighing. As quickly and as quietly as she could, Sharon made her way to the crossroads. Every few paces she stopped and listened, peering carefully about her. Nothing. Nobody. She couldn't even hear the sea. Must mean the tide was out. There was some way you could tell the time from the tide. Neddie had explained it. But she couldn't remember how.

At the crossroads, she stopped. She could hear the sea now. The soft lapping of the waves on the sand, far away. No other sound. No barking from the barns. She shivered and wished she'd brought Teddy.

Sharon turned into the Ridgeway. Quiet going for a while on a grassy path, but after a couple of hundred metres she reached the shingle and stone drive. No lights in the bungalows. Good – it must be late. She scurried along the edge of the driveway, like a mouse along a skirting board.

Bleedin' 'ell, what was that!

A car! Coming up the Ridgeway. Headlights. They were bound to see her. Couple more bends in the road and they'd be on her. No trees. No ditch. Nothing to hide in.

Hang about. Hang about! Quick, quick! Up there – gap between the bungalows.

Sharon darted up the slope and threw herself down, just as the car headlights flashed round the bend. The car was moving slowly. Late night revellers returning from a party, or a club, or a disco. In a few seconds, the car had crunched past her and was out of sight.

She heard the car come to a halt. Doors slam. Voices. Footsteps. Silence.

Sharon hurried to the end of the Ridgeway and crossed the field. Her eyes were now well accustomed to the dark, and she could make out the gap in the line of hedge round the caravan park. The 'back door' she had used in her flight after smashing the windscreen of Joanne and Ben's car.

Good. No lights in any of the caravans. No movement. No sounds. She slipped between the caravans, making her way towards The Stores.

Not far now, and good and dark. No street lights, and both bulbs gone in the public telephones by the Park entrance. Well done, the hooligans.

She reached The Stores. OK, so far.

Round the back. That was the place. Big windows. Well hidden from the road. Piles of empty crates and boxes to duck behind if anyone should suddenly turn up.

This was it, then. Like going to the dentist. Come on, Sharon, open wide. Except that the window won't open wide. You'll have to smash it and chance the noise. The important thing was to keep the glass covered. Put a cloth over it, and then try to break a corner.

Sharon unzipped her jacket, and took the knife from her sock. She held the jacket against the glass and began tapping, holding the knife by the blade.

What a row! And she was being ever so gentle. No good. Have to hit it harder, then. Fetch it a clout. No point in making a noise and not breaking the window.

Still no good.

How hard did you have to hit this window? Better get something heavier than the knife. And get a move on. Didn't do to waste time. There were plenty of large stones in the car park. Sharon selected one. Again, she held her jacket against the glass.

Thump!

This time there was a cracking, splintering sound. Sharon froze. She waited for lights to flick on. Or the sound of caravan doors opening. People hurrying over. The dreaded: 'What's going on?'

But there was nothing. She relaxed her arm, and took her jacket from the window. The glass was sufficiently split for her to be able to lever out small pieces from the corner, using her knife point. Now she needed to knock out more glass, to make a hole big enough to squeeze through. She enlarged the hole until she could get her hand in. Then, wrapping her jacket round her hand, she held on to the glass, and began loosening larger pieces. As each piece became loose, she removed it, and carefully placed it on the ground.

Nearly done. Few more bits.

Here's a big one. Don't drop it.

Jeez! What was that!

A cat darted from under the hedge and streaked across the car park. Somehow Sharon held on to the jagged glass until her hands stopped shaking, and it was safe for her to add it to the pile on the ground. That would do. The hole was big enough. Now for it. Done the breaking bit: now the entering. She climbed slowly, taking care to avoid the sharp edges of the broken window.

Once in, she dropped down immediately behind one of the shelf units, on all fours, muscles tensed, ready to leg it back through the window if there was any danger.

There were no sounds, save for the steady hum of the electric motors in the freezer chests.

By the check-out there was a pile of boxes.

Sharon crawled across the floor, chose a box and crawled back. She pushed the box through the hole in the window. Towel first. Lay that on the bottom of the box and then the bottles of mineral water won't clink. She grabbed an orange and red towel from a pile in the corner.

Back to the window. She placed the towel in the box. Mineral water next. Two bottles at a time. She daren't risk more. Six bottles in all. She couldn't carry more. Soluble aspirin. Where would that be? On the shelf behind the magazine counter.

Sun-tan lotion . . . insect repellant . . . indigestion tablets . . . Ah! Soluble aspirin. And there was toothpaste. And toothbrushes. She darted back to the broken window.

Was that all? Towel, water, aspirin, toothpaste? Big time crime! All that worry and risk, for some water and a chance to clean your teeth. She had one last look round, and picked up a box of milk chocolates. An' all because the lady loves Milk Tray . . .

She climbed out, picked up her jacket and put it on. As she did so, a small piece of paper fluttered from one of the pockets to the ground. Sharon didn't notice it. She was off. Across the wet grass, through the caravan park. Quickly. Silently. Making for the gap. There she paused, partly for breath, partly to put the box down and give her arms a rest, and partly to make sure there was no one about.

All clear.

She rubbed her arms. This was no joke. What a weight! But a couple of days and she'd have to be back for more. It *was* like going to the dentist, and then the dentist saying: 'You'll have to make another appointment for more fillings.'

Sharon picked up the box, and crossed the field. She trudged along the Ridgeway, stopping to rest every few minutes. There were no more scares. No lights, no noise, no cars. She reached the shack, drank half a bottle of mineral water, grabbed her teddy, and curled up in her plastic and cardboard bed.

For a while she couldn't get to sleep. There were too many questions her mind couldn't answer. Would the police trace her? What about The Laurels? And the barns? Joanne and Ben – when were they coming down again?

Outside the wind freshened. The tide was still coming in, and the onshore breeze stirred the leaves in the wood. The dead stalks of maize clapped in the nearby field. The wind blew stronger, whipping across the pits, racing across the bay, nipping between the caravans in the park.

The piece of paper Sharon had dropped in the yard behind The Stores flapped and lifted. A gust caught it and carried it to the hedge. Here it stuck, a few metres from the broken window.

The questions dropped unanswered from Sharon's mind. With a little moan of weariness and misery, she tightened her hold on Teddy and fell asleep.

Chapter Fourteen

'Thought it might be a bit quieter, now the season's over,' said the local policeman. 'Much taken? What were they after? Cash from the till?'

'No,' said the owner of The Stores. 'All that mess and damage for a towel and a box of chocolates. No sense in it.'

'My colleagues will be coming from Rye. The professionals. Fingerprint powder, magnifying glasses, bloodhounds – the lot. Still, while I'm here, I'll have a look round. Try not to stamp me size twelves on anything that's too important.'

He looked at the broken window.

'Someone small, whoever he was. Kid, most likely.'

'That's what I thought,' said the owner. 'But what's a kid want with a towel?'

'And there's been no money taken? Well, let's have a look inside.'

The policeman followed the owner into the shop, and gazed around.

'There's not a lot of mess,' he said. 'Unless you've tidied it up.'

'There's enough mess,' said the owner, stubbornly. 'Knocking the bottles about, over there, by the soft drinks. And the pharmaceuticals.'

'Not drugs, though,' said the policeman. 'You don't stock drugs, do you? That's something kids *do* go for.'

'What? – fruit-salts, plasters, aspirins? That sort of thing? No, I tell you, it makes no sense.'

The policeman looked at her. It was part of his job to be as stubborn as she was.

'In the end it always does make sense. Some sort of sense.' Again, he looked about him. 'Got in there – by breaking the window – that's clear enough. Where was the towel?'

The owner pointed. 'In the corner.'

'So, he snatched up a towel. Maybe dropped it. That could be how this counter got disturbed. Then – back to the window, grabbing the box of chocs on the way.'

A police car pulled up behind The Stores.

'Now we can leave it to the experts,' said the local policeman.

He nodded as another policeman and a policewoman entered the shop, and introduced them to the owner.

'Not much to it,' he said. 'Little taken. Bit of damage. Looks like a kid, or kids. Some time last night, probably early this morning. Nobody heard anything. Nobody's reported seeing anything.'

'OK,' said the Rye policeman. 'We'll take over.'

'Left the bloodhound in the car, have you?' said the local policeman. 'Got plenty to drink, has he? Don't want him passing out with dehydration. Don't want the RSPCA in.'

'Very witty,' said the Rye policeman. 'Time you got back on lollipop duty, isn't it?'

'Yes. Mustn't be late. Miss me mark in the register.' The local man nodded to the owner and left.

The two officers from Rye were thorough. They examined the broken window, searching for any scraps of material on the jagged edges of the glass. They made notes.

'And you're certain that's all that's missing? Just a towel and chocolates?'

'There may be one or two things,' said the owner. 'I haven't checked the entire stock.'

'Nothing missing here, where you've got the toiletries and medicines?'

'There may be, but it can't be much. I'd have noticed.'

The policewoman pointed to the soft drinks. 'Somebody's had a bit of a go here,' she said.

'Fetched it a kick on his way out. Just for spite,' said the owner. 'Kids!'

'It's not really on his way out,' said the policeman.

'Or *her* way out,' said the policewoman.

'Women's lib,' said the policeman, to the owner, out of the corner of his mouth. 'Won't let us men take the credit for anything. Even crime.'

'You're sure nothing's missing from here?'

'Hard to tell,' said the owner. 'Well – yes. I think there's some mineral water gone. I always keep a dozen or so bottles. It's become popular lately. Often get asked for it. Yes, looks like several bottles gone.'

'Towel, chocolates, mineral water,' said the policeman. 'Midnight beach party for total abstainers.'

'And possibly some medicines. Aspirin, something like that,' said the policewoman.

'Somebody taken ill in the middle of the night?'

'You don't want chocolates when you're ill.'

'I do,' said the policeman.

'Somebody come away without packing properly,' said the policewoman. 'Sort of things a man would forget – essentials.'

'Chocolates aren't essential,' said the policeman. 'Nor is mineral water.' He didn't like the criticism of his sex.

'Water could be. Somebody camping too far from a tap.'

'Camping? This time of year?' said the policeman.

'Someone desperate, then,' said the policewoman. 'A kid, possibly. Someone with no money. Remember that crack the local bobby made about our bloodhound? Someone getting thirsty. With no water supply. Someone hiding.'

The policeman turned to the owner. 'We'll take a look outside. You needn't bother. You'll be getting customers soon.'

The two police officers left The Stores and walked to the yard at the back, where the crates and empty boxes were stacked.

'I was talking to this bloke from Kent, the other night,' said the policeman, 'and he said there's a lot of chatter their way about a drugs' ring. Nothing definite. But Romney Marsh is being mentioned. Coastguards at Lydd and Folkestone are working with them. And Customs.'

'What's that got to do with this? Don't see a drugs' ring being responsible for this. It's too . . . too domestic,' said the policewoman.

She looked about her. In the hedge was the scrap of paper that had fluttered from Sharon's jacket. The policeman saw it, too.

'Keep Britain tidy,' he said.

He picked it up, and began to crumple it in his hand.

'You might as well have a look at it,' said the policewoman, with a smile. 'It might be a clue.'

The policeman looked.

'169, Cornwall Road, Forest Hill,' he read. 'Yes,' he said. 'It might be a clue.'

Chapter Fifteen

Breakfast on Friday morning at Cornwall Road was not a comfortable affair, as far as Joanne was concerned. The row her parents were having was largely her fault.

'Are you saying that you want us to go back to that blessed caravan tonight?'

Dad looked at Mum. 'It's the only place the cheque card can be. I've looked everywhere else.'

'Is our caravan really blessed?' said Ben, in between mouthfuls of toast.

Joanne hardly heard him. She'd caused this row. She'd behaved like a criminal, hiding Dad's cheque card, taking it from his coat while everyone else was putting bags in the car.

But at least it would get them back to Winchelsea. She could check, to see if Sharon was safe. If there was any doubt about it, Joanne had decided she would tell Mum and Dad. About Sharon. And they would tell the police, of that she was certain, and the police would take Sharon back to her home.

And quite right, too! Anything else was ridiculous. The risks Sharon was taking!

And if she discovered Sharon was OK?

Joanne almost hoped Sharon wasn't OK. Then the whole silly adventure would come to an end. The barns?

The man on the motor-bike? Part of life's mysteries. No more important than Mum and Dad wondering how Irene, next door, could afford such expensive new curtains.

'It's just that you said "blessed". I thought maybe a saint had once lived in it. Or a hermit. Or a relic.'

'Relic?'

Ben had managed to get his mother involved.

'Relics don't live anywhere,' she said.

'That's awful,' said Ben. 'Nowhere to live.'

'Don't be ridiculous. A relic is a bit of old bone, or wood, or scrap of material. It isn't a person.'

'About the card,' began Dad.

'Then if a relic never lived there, what made our caravan "blessed"? Was anyone martyred there?'

'You might be.'

Joanne joined in. 'Yes,' she said, 'one of the early Christians was thrown to the sea-lions.'

Ben stuck out his tongue.

'That reminds me,' said Mum. 'Go and clean your teeth.'

Ben left the room. Mum turned back to Dad.

'I take it *I'm* expected to ask Irene to feed the cat and turn up the heating in the greenhouse.'

'Irene won't mind,' said Dad. 'She'll love a nose round. And it's only for one night.'

'I suppose it may give Jo a chance to meet her secret admirer.'

There was a crash. A plate had slipped from Joanne's grasp.

'Sorry,' she said. 'I'll get the dustpan.'

This was getting beyond a joke. Joanne swept up the

broken pieces as quickly as she could, and silently prayed there'd be no more jokes about secrets.

Mum and Dad said nothing, but Joanne had seen the brief glance they exchanged.

Ben returned.

'Are we going down to the caravan?' he said.

'We are.'

'Will I miss "It's a Knockout"?'

'Don't blame me,' said Mum.

'At least you now know what a martyr is,' said Dad.

'Don't encourage him in this nonsense,' said Mum. 'Have you got your packed lunch?'

Ben nodded.

'And your PE kit?'

Ben nodded.

'Did you brush your teeth?'

Ben breathed peppermint fumes in everyone's direction.

'I'll get back from school as quick as I can,' said Joanne. 'Give you a hand with the packing.'

'It's all right. Your father can give me a hand when he gets back from work. That'll teach him not to be so careless with his blessed cheque card.'

Mum and Dad looked at Ben.

He opened his mouth, but said nothing.

Joanne didn't join in the laughter.

They left the house at half past five, and drove slowly through Bromley in the Friday night rush hour. It was getting dark, and clouds were gathering, as they put on more speed along the Sevenoaks by-pass.

At twenty past six, a police car drew up in Cornwall

Road. The driver reported his arrival on his radio, got out of the car and walked to the front door of 169.

He knocked and waited. Curtains twitched next door.

The policeman knocked again, stepped back, and peered at the house.

'Excuse me . . .'

It was Irene, the neighbour, cat food in one hand, watering can in the other. 'Are you looking for Mr and Mrs Lewis?'

'Family that lives here?'

'Yes, that's right. They're not in. They've gone away for the weekend. Down to their new caravan at Winchelsea Beach. Sussex. They left nearly an hour ago. I expect you could catch them if you hurried.'

'You think they might be fleeing the country?'

'Oh, no. They're going to Winchelsea.'

We can't all have a sense of humour, thought the policeman.

'No need for a hue and cry, then,' he said. 'They'll be back on Monday?'

'Before then, I imagine. Sunday afternoon. Because of the children.' Irene was craning her neck, this way and that, eager for any crumb that the policeman threw to her.

'Children?'

'Yes. Joanne and Ben. Nice children. Not the sort I should have expected to be in any sort of trouble.'

The policeman said nothing.

'Are they in any sort of trouble?' asked Irene, hopefully.

'I doubt it, madam,' said the policeman. 'Was the family here last night?'

'Oh yes.'

'And the children?'

'Oh yes.'

The policeman looked at her. She was clutching the tin of cat food and the watering can. He wondered whether she intended to feed the cat or give him a bath.

'Shall I tell them you called?'

'No, that's all right, thank you, madam. We'll get in touch. Next week.'

The policeman trotted down the path, back to his car. He sat at the driving wheel, but didn't start up the engine. Instead, he spoke into his radio.

'Nobody here. The president of Neighbourhood Watch, who lives next door, says the family weren't at the caravan during the week . . . yes . . . yes, they've got a caravan on the site . . . I should pass the information back to Sussex . . . it's down to them now . . . doesn't seem to be any sort of lead to that break-in, but if Sussex want to check it out, the family will be back at their caravan tonight. Within the next couple of hours, at a guess.'

The policeman signed off, and reached forward to turn on the ignition. He noticed Irene, still at the front door, still staring at him. Probably been trying to lip read what he had said. He gave her the briefest of smiles and drove off.

Irene went inside, wondering which of her friends to telephone first. Not a lot happened in her life.

It started to rain.

Chapter Sixteen

Sharon slept late on Friday morning, worn out by the burglary of the night before. She woke suddenly, sharply, as though something was wrong. She couldn't tell what, but she was sore, aching, uncomfortable, and uneasy. She sat up in her bed of cardboard boxes and looked about her.

There was the box from last night. Trouble, that would mean. Bound to bring the police in. And suppose somebody *had* seen her? It was possible.

She should have left The Stores well alone.

Oh yes? And go without water? And keep getting dirtier and dirtier? Got no option: had to get those things.

Sharon crawled from her dosser's bed and stood up. She rubbed her aching legs and hips. Eight nights she'd spent on the floor of the shack. Eight long, cold, lonely, miserable nights. She was dirty and desperate. This couldn't go on much longer.

But what else was she to do?

How easy it would be to give herself up. There was a police station in Rye. Neddie had once threatened to drag her there, yonks ago. She'd only to walk into Rye, tell them who she was, and leave the rest to them. They'd sort it out. She'd be back at The Laurels in a couple of hours.

But – there was last night's break-in to think of. Juvenile court, that'd be. Like Carol's brother. And he got detention centre. No, thank you very much.

No need for the Old Bill. She could get herself back to The Laurels. Hop on a train. Even buy a ticket, if need be. Jim'd help her. He'd pay for the damage, and the stuff she'd nicked. Wouldn't be the first time. And then she could have a bath, and go to bed. Jim would see she was tired. He'd see she was grubby.

Grubby? She was *filthy*. She could bear it no longer. She must have a clean-up. First her teeth. She brushed them carefully, with her stolen toothbrush and mineral water. That was better, but what she needed most of all was a bath.

She grabbed her towel and hurried along the path to the beach. She climbed the sea-wall and dropped on to the shingle. It was a cold day, cloudy, with a threat of rain, and the wind gusting from the west. The tide was miles out. She plunged down the shingle and on to the wet, brown sand. There was no one about. Sharon felt alone in the world, and shuddered.

She ran across the sand, heading for the sea. By the water's edge, she stripped to her underwear, and then waded in.

She almost screamed with cold.

It took her ages to reach water deep enough to splash in, let alone swim, and during that time she became colder and colder, the water carving slices off her body. She splashed about, rubbing her arms and legs, forcing herself to duck her head under.

Two minutes was enough.

Back to the sand to grab the towel.

Fool! It was damp. She should have been more careful. She rubbed her body vigorously, and did what she could to dry her hair. Her clothes, too, had soaked up water from the sand, and felt cold and clammy on her body. She dressed rapidly and hurried from the beach. The plunge had done little to raise her spirits.

Breakfast. That was what she wanted. Sausages and fried eggs. Fried bread. Sugar Puffs. Hot chocolate. Toast and butter. Jim used to do good breakfasts, at the weekend.

He was all right, Jim.

She ran all the way back to the shack, and opened yet another tin of cold baked beans. After two spoonfuls, she gave up, and ate a consolation handful of milk chocolates.

She thought about the day. Better avoid The Stores. The Old Bill might be there. Stay away from the caravan park altogether. Better not go for chicken and chips tonight, either. That meant a long walk to Rye for hot food.

Oh, well, sort that out later. What about now?

The barns. Go and have a look round there.

The dogs were barking.

She didn't know what time it was, but reckoned it must be gone dinner-time. So 'Wally' would have been already.

She'd go and have a look round now. She crammed her pockets with more chocolates, and set off through the wood.

She skirted the shores of the gravel pits, and reached the last piece of cover before she would have to cross open country. Here was a narrow neck of land, a stony path, separating two of the pits. This was risky. Open water on both sides of the path, and not a tree, not a bush, not so much as a clump of cow-parsley, between her and the barbed-wire fence. And on the other side of the fence was the cart track that led past the barns.

The barns. Long and low. Metal and concrete. The shed, with the curved roof, arched like the tunnel of a toy train-set. An abandoned air about all three buildings. Piles of wood. Bales of rotting straw. Rusting farm machinery.

Sharon took one last look, and sprinted over the stretch of open land. She nipped between the strands of barbed-wire.

So far, so good.

Now then, what was old Wally up to?

She squeezed past bales of straw and entered the first of the barns. It was warm inside. That was a pleasant surprise. Warm and dry. And a nice old smell. Straw, warm wood, creosote. Dusty, but not so's it made you cough.

For all the notices and warnings, there was no sign of anything interesting or valuable, let alone mysterious. More bales of straw and stacks of wood, that was all.

Try the other barn.

This was piled from floor to roof with wooden crates, full of potatoes. Didn't make a lot of sense, leaving them all here. Frost would get them soon.

Perhaps something out of the ordinary *was* taking place.

But what?

What was all the fuss about? All the dogs and tape-recorders and bits of wire she'd seen through the window of the shed? For the life of her, she couldn't see anything criminal in a load of old boxes, straw and spuds.

Try the shed, then.

The roughly-painted door was padlocked, like last time. So Sharon went to the window at the other end, where there was a convenient gate propped against the wall. She stood on the middle bar of the gate, and pressed her nose against the dirty glass. Couldn't hardly see a thing. She must have struck luckier that other time. Course! The sun had been shining then, lighting up the inside a bit. No sun today, so it was pitch dark inside the shed.

Have to get in.

It was like a self-dare, and she never refused a dare.

Out with the knife. Getting used to breaking and entering. She removed the entire window pane, placed it on the ground by the gate, and climbed in.

And, all the time, the dogs barked on.

Again, a strong smell. Not so nice, though. Musty. Cobwebby. Ancient. Sort of place you'd expect to trip over something dead. Or have a rat run up your trouser-leg.

Now then, where was that old bench that ran down the side of the shed? The one with the gadgets on? Ah, there it was. Her hand found it. Her eyes became accustomed to the darkness, and she could see coils of wire, and batteries, and tools, and –

'Bleedin' 'ell!

Bleedin' knee, more like.

She had tripped over something on the floor. Was it something dead? She crouched down, and felt with her hand.

It didn't take long to discover what had caused her fall. A football. It was like Joanne and Ben said. Footballs. Everywhere, footballs.

What for?

Gingerly, she put her hand to her left knee. It really did hurt. She could have broken her leg, going over like that. And she'd crashed into the bench, and must have knocked something important over, 'cos the dogs had gone ever so quiet.

Her little pink hand grabbed the bench, and she pulled herself up. She searched for the tape-recorder.

There it was. Still going round, but there wasn't anything like enough noise coming from it. Old Wally would never hear that. Wouldn't scare anyone off, either. She turned the volume up as high as it would go. Still no good. There was a loose lead. The plug must have come out of the loudspeaker.

Well, best not waste time looking for it. Not hang about – in case Wally came to investigate.

But first: what else had we got 'ere? Money? No, even wallies don't keep money in sheds. Stolen property? Could be. Maybe the spuds were stolen. Art treasures? Neddie had once told her about how people smuggle pictures and antiques across to Europe from the south coast.

But it didn't seem likely. Jim had told her about old paintings. You had to look after them. Keep the temperature right.

No, paintings and furniture seemed out of it.

And why the electrics?

Sharon swept her hand once more along the workbench. Coils of thin, plastic covered wire. Very short lengths. Looked a bit like Dolly Mixtures. And pieces of plastic card. Like credit cards. And there were needles, and things that looked like tweezers. And was that a soldering-iron? And a bicycle pump. It didn't make no sort of sense. Unless that was for the footballs.

Footballs.

Plastic footballs. A whole crate of them. The sort that kids muck about with. The sort Jim said was costing him a fortune at The Laurels.

Didn't make sense. Footballs? What was it? – the secret training headquarters of Wallies United? Joanne and Ben said that Wally had a football with him on his motorbike, the other day. And hadn't they said something about another wally kicking a football into the sea? So, what were the wallies up to? Smuggling plastic footballs? That was big crime, all right. And smuggling them the hard way: kicking them into the sea, and hoping the tide would take them to France or Holland.

She didn't know how near the truth she was.

What was that?

Motor. Motor-bike. Wally. Must be Wally. Coming this way. Missed his doggies. Coming to investigate.

Sharon's mind raced, but it was instinct that told her what to do. Leg it. She'd got to leg it. Any minute now, Wally'd be in through that door, so she'd better get out the window – smartish.

The motor-bike slowed down, and stopped. The engine ticked over. The engine was switched off. By then Sharon had leapt through the window, jumped from the gate, and was peering round the side of the shed. She could see the motor-bike, parked in the space at the front of the barns.

Another quick look round. No one in sight. But she could hear voices. Wally had a mate with him. She heard someone fitting a key into the padlock of the shed door.

That was it. Away she fled, darting over the track, throwing herself over the barbed-wire fence, and racing between the flooded gravel pits.

Must reach that bit of wood, by the fields. Before they saw her. With every second stride, the bruised knee shot pain into her, but there was no time to heed it.

Once, twice, she looked over her shoulder.

The second time – there, they hadn't wasted any time. Wally and his mate, getting back on the motor-bike. And in a hurry. They must have seen her. The hope was, it would take them some time to get the bike over that barbed-wire.

She sped on, and reached the outskirts of the wood. She heard the bike start up, an angry, savage roar, powerful and fearsome. Again she looked back – but Wally and his mate weren't coming her way. They were following the track, parallel to hers, heading for the crossroads. Picking up the traces from last time. Wally must have remembered the general direction in which she had headed with Joanne and Ben.

It only needed the motor-bike to turn right when it got to the crossroads, and she was done for.

The bike drew ahead of her. Sometimes she lost sight of it, for there was an embankment on the far side of the gravel pit. But then the track climbed towards the crossroads – and she saw it turn right.

The shack wasn't far now. She'd get there first. It was home. It was a chance. Maybe she could hide there.

Maybe they wouldn't find it. She plunged through the sodden clumps of wet grass, sending up sprays of water, almost falling as her feet caught in bramble shoots, ducking low under branches of willow, squeezing between ash saplings.

The bike had left the path, and was crossing the field of winter wheat. Sharon could see the stalks flattened to left and right by the heavy machine.

She did reach the shack first, by a couple of minutes. She was gasping, and panting, and very, very frightened. She risked peeping through the window. The bike swung into the clearing in front of the shack. It slowed. Stopped. The engine was cut.

Silence.

Wally and his mate sat astride the bike, staring at the shack.

Sharon was too exhausted to run any further. It would take hours to recover her strength. Her stamina had gone, and her control was on the verge of collapse. For a moment she thought she would be sick, wet herself and burst into tears, all at the same time.

Wally's mate got off the bike. The two men talked.

What were they going to do? Burst in and beat her up? Kill her? It wouldn't take much: they could simply walk in and grab her.

The man moved from the bike. Wally started the engine, and accelerated away, out of the clearing, back the way he had come.

The other man, rarely taking his eyes from the shack, moved to the edge of the clearing, and leant against a tree. He took a packet of cigarettes and a lighter from his pocket. He stayed by the tree, smoking and watching.

Sharon shrank back from the window, but she felt he could still see her.

It started to rain, but the watcher under the tree showed no signs of leaving. It looked to Sharon as though he was ready for a long wait.

And then what?

A beating?

Or something worse?

Chapter Seventeen

The rain had driven all the children inside at The Laurels. They had finished their tea, and were slumped round the television set, watching 'It's a Knockout'.

The phone rang.

Jim signalled to Terry that he would go and answer it. Carol clattered after him, but paused at the doorway of his office.

Jim picked up the receiver.

'Hallo, Ruth,' he said.

He beckoned Carol in to join him. She could hear only Jim's side of the conversation.

'Yes . . . But no trace of Neddie? . . . I see . . . I don't know. I might . . . Yes, I suppose so . . . I'd like to think about that. Thanks for phoning. 'Bye.'

Jim replaced the receiver.

'They haven't found Sharon?' said Carol.

'No, but there is some news about Neddie. He *did* have a boat, and it was moored down at Rye. He used to take children down there. Rye Harbour.'

'What are you going to do?'

'I'm thinking about that.'

Carol was old enough to let him think. She stood, watching him, half guessing, half feeling what was going on in his mind. She wondered if it had occurred to him that he might never see Sharon again. It had occurred to

Carol. She had imagined all manner of harm that Sharon might have come to. And, for the last two days, she'd faced the thought that maybe Sharon was gone for good.

What would happen then? What would Jim do? What would any of them do? When had anybody last seen Sharon? What was the last thing she had said to Sharon? What did Sharon look like? Carol felt that she was beginning to forget.

'Come on,' she said, abruptly. 'You got petrol in your car?'

Jim looked up. 'A trip to Rye?'

'Course!'

'I could simply telephone the police, and pass the information on to them.'

'Which would you rather do?'

Jim sighed. 'It's a long time since anyone said that to me, Carol. I think I'd rather go down to Rye myself.'

'Thought you would. But someone better go with you: look after you.' Carol couldn't keep a trace of pleasure out of her voice.

'Would you like to tell Linda to do my duty for me?'

'No, I wouldn't!'

'Didn't think so. I'll do it. And I'd better telephone Mrs Bathurst.'

'Want to do that on your own?'

Carol grinned and left the office.

She stood in the hall, watching the rain fall on the dark driveway outside. From time to time, she could hear Jim's voice. He spoke loudly: it sounded as though he was losing his temper. She couldn't catch any of the words, but she heard the receiver slam down.

Jim came out.

'We off, then? To Rye?'

'We are,' he said.

'Got to. Only thing to do.'

He looked grateful for that.

'We'll find her,' said Carol.

'It's not likely,' said Jim. 'Hundred to one against. Thousand, maybe. Do you still want to come?'

'I think I'd better,' said Carol. 'You look dreadful. And I'll have fifty pence at a hundred to one.'

She was surprised at how pleased she felt.

As they went out to Jim's car together, ten minutes later, leaving a disgruntled Linda looking after a group of disgruntled children, Jim said: 'And all the time, Carol, I bet Sharon's sitting somewhere safe, and warm, and dry, and laughing at you and me, and The Laurels, and Ruth, and the whole damn pack of us.'

'Ten to one she isn't,' said Carol.

Chapter Eighteen

The rain thudded on the roof of the shack. It slid off the greasy windows. Through the smears and blots, Sharon could just see the watcher, under the trees. From time to time he lit a cigarette, stamped his feet, pulled the collar of his coat tighter around his neck.

Normally, Sharon would have laughed at someone in his position. Stuck out there, getting soaked, waiting for hours, and all because of her. But not on this occasion.

The hours passed. Sharon hardly dared move. Her leg had stiffened. Now and then she rubbed it, gently. Didn't make a lot of difference: she was still too exhausted to do a runner.

She was hungry. She'd eaten nothing since the cold baked beans and the chocolates after her swim. There wasn't much food to choose from. She tried nibbling a biscuit. It was damp and crumbly. It tasted foul. She spat the bits out and searched for something else. There were still chocolates in her jacket pocket. She fished a couple out, but, like her, they'd been bruised by her fall in the shed, and they looked unappetising. She didn't fancy the way her hand was shaking, either. What she did fancy was something hot and delicious – like a steamed pudding with jam sauce and ladles of creamy custard. She could see it in her mind, smell it, almost hear the scrape of spoon on plate.

She found a tin of peaches and ate them, slowly, and with no enjoyment.

He was still there – the watcher. Under the trees. She could see the glow of his cigarette.

The rain increased. It grew darker. Sharon shivered, partly from cold, largely from fear. She reckoned 'they' were waiting for the dark. The watcher. Wally. Others as well, probably.

Something would happen as soon as it got dark.

She was starting on her third fingernail, when she heard the noise of a motor. Not the bike, a deeper sound. A heavier vehicle. 'They' were running a risk, bringing a motor out here, over that field.

By pressing her nose against the window, Sharon could make out the flickering of sidelights behind the screen of trees. There was no glare of headlights: it was impossible to tell where the motor was heading. Instead, the tiny, teasing lights seemed more like will-o'-the-wisps. Magic. Wicked. The vehicle came to rest in the gap in the trees, facing the shack. The lights were switched off. Sharon saw the outline of a van, about the size of the minibus Jim hired for holidays.

Jim. Where was he? Miles away. Enjoying himself.

The watcher had been expecting the van. He crossed briskly to it and opened the back doors. Two men emerged. The driver stayed where he was. The watcher led the other two men to the tree where he had been sheltering. Sharon saw him point to the shack. It didn't take a genius to work out they were making some sort of plan.

The men spread out. They were going to surround her. Now, suddenly, far too late, Sharon felt a surge of energy return to her limbs. She should have bunked it hours ago – given that watcher a run for his money. Get away – anywhere. Farm, bungalow, pub, shop. Up the main road. Get a car to stop.

But it was too late now. Already she'd lost sight of two of the men. She could see only the watcher, making straight for her.

Too late to run. What then? Hide? Couldn't. Get hold of some weapon?

Like what? Bottle? Yeah, that mineral water.

Where? In the cupboard. Quick, quick!

Bleedin' 'ell! They was 'ere already. Someone at the back, trying the doors.

Sharon grabbed two bottles. Her frightened eyes darted to and fro. Where best to go? Behind the door? And what then?

Depended what way they came at her. Chuck the bottle? Or use it as a club?

She crouched by the cupboard, her right hand grasping a full bottle of mineral water by the neck. In her left hand she had one of the empties. She could hear sounds of movement at the front and back of the shack. Low voices. Muttering. The hissing intake of breath. There was nothing she could do, but wait.

She didn't have to wait long. There was a sharp crack as one of the rear windows was smashed, and, at the same time, the door at the front of the shack was wrenched open. The watcher stood in the doorway.

'Come on, sonny,' he said, but there was no affection in his voice. 'Let's be having you.'

There was the sound of more breaking glass, and a head appeared at the window.

'Get a move on,' said the watcher. 'He's in here someplace.' Then, as he peered into the darkness, again the words: 'Come on, sonny.'

Sharon could bear it no longer. In a primitive burst for survival, a cornered animal in the cramped kitchen, she hurled herself into the attack. The full bottle she threw, fiercely, at the head in the window. For once she missed her target, and the bottle smashed against the wall, shattering and spraying mineral water in all directions. With the empty bottle, she rushed at the watcher, hoping to kill him.

The bottle caught him on the shoulder, angering him, but doing no physical damage. From then on, the fight was bitter, but short. Sharon stood no chance against three grown men, as she knew from past experience, when she'd freaked out in children's homes. But she put up a brave and wild struggle to save herself. She bit, scratched and pinched. In her terror, she was unable to distinguish one attacker from another. Their forms merged into one massive, six-armed creature, like a mythical monster. But whatever she saw, she kicked or punched. And she spat.

No words were spoken. The only sounds were of furniture splintering, and glass being crunched underfoot. Sharon never cried out. The men never shouted. It was like a dumb nightmare, some mute, terrifying dream, that came to an abrupt halt when they slammed her against the wall, knocking all the wind and fight out of her.

Only then did one of the men speak.

'Bloody little rat.'

He was nursing his hand, some of the skin from which was under the few fingernails Sharon hadn't bitten earlier that afternoon.

'Bloody little rat. I'll kill you.'

Chapter Nineteen

It was too late to reach Sharon tonight. It was dark, it was cold, and the rain was swirling in from the sea and splattering against the caravan.

Joanne felt helpless. She wished they'd stayed in London. Mum was complaining about the weather. Dad was moaning about his cheque card. In a minute, Joanne felt, she'd have to tell him where to look.

They had nearly finished their supper. Joanne scraped the last of the tinned rice-pudding out of her bowl.

There was a knock on the caravan door. A loud knock.

Dad went to the door. As it opened outwards, Joanne was unable to see the caller, but she heard the voice clearly enough.

'Mr Lewis?' A strong voice, confident, official.

'Yes.'

'I'm WPC McGowan, from Rye police. Could I come in?'

Dad stood by the door, and held out his arm to usher in a policewoman.

'Not the best of weekend weather, is it?' she said. 'May I sit down?'

'Of course.' Dad was at once flustered.

The policewoman sat on the bench seat opposite Joanne, and next to Ben. She smiled at them both.

The Shack by the Sea 125

Something's happened to Sharon, thought Joanne. Something awful. She's had an accident. She's ill. She's dead. She's been found dead, and it's all my fault for keeping the secret.

But then self-concern asserted itself. It wasn't her fault. It was Sharon's fault. *She'd* run away from the home. *She'd* gone to live in the shack. *She* was the one who turned people's lives upside down.

There wasn't time to think more along those lines. The policewoman held a piece of paper in her hand. The paper was grubby and crumpled. She passed it to Dad.

'Is this your address in London, Mr Lewis?'

Dad looked at the piece of paper and nodded.

'It's not your writing?' said the policewoman. This time Dad shook his head. The policewoman passed the paper to Joanne.

'Did you write this?'

Joanne felt her limbs begin to tremble. No, it wasn't her writing. But she recognised the piece of paper. The image flashed into her mind of the eager Sharon, stub of pencil in one hand, crumpled paper in the other, scribbling their address and promising to write.

'No.' It was a very husky 'no'.

Ben glanced at his sister's unhappy face. He said nothing. Joanne didn't blame him.

At this point, in plays and films, she thought, somebody says: 'May I ask what all this is about?' But nobody did.

There was a pause.

The policewoman passed the paper to Ben.

'Did you write this?'

Her voice was kind, and she was smiling. Ben didn't even look up.

'No,' he said. 'No, thank you.'

The policewoman laughed. 'I'll explain,' she said. 'We found this piece of paper this morning, in the hedge behind The Stores. There was a break-in there, last night. It's all right, we know it wasn't you. But we like to check these things out. Have you any idea who did write this?'

Ben had taken his watch off, and was playing with the buttons, altering the display panels.

The policewoman was looking at Joanne.

Joanne wished she wasn't the older one. And lots more: she wished she hadn't been brought up to tell the truth, and that she didn't feel so desperately worried about Sharon, and that Mum and Dad weren't looking at her.

She didn't know what to say. This was the moment she had feared. The moment when someone asked directly about Sharon. It was all too complicated. Her mind couldn't keep up with it all. She was about to say that she did know who wrote it, but suddenly realised that the policewoman wasn't simply asking: 'Who wrote the address?' She was asking: 'Who broke into The Stores?' It was like rescuing Sharon from one danger, and shoving her into another.

At that point, her mind switched off, and she focused her eyes on the face of Ben's watch. She saw the seconds blink by, flashed on the display . . . 37 . . . 38 . . . 39 . . . 40 . . .

It was Mum who took charge.

'Who was it, love?'

Joanne started to cry. She could hold on no longer. She'd tried to do right by Sharon, to keep her promise and Sharon's secret. She'd tried to help. But it had all got worse and worse. Danger, damage, deceit. Now it was crime, and this runaway, tearaway girl was forcing her to decide whether it was going to be children's home or prison or maybe death in the shack.

It was that final thought, the last she reckoned she was capable of before collapse, that decided her.

It really was a matter of life or death. And Joanne decided that Sharon must live.

'It was Sharon,' she whispered.

Mum scuttled round to her side. The policewoman leant forward in her seat. Dad stood, frozen to the spot. One touch of her mother's hand on her shoulder, and Joanne began to shake with her longing for comfort. Nobody hurried her. They let her cry – there was plenty of time.

Gradually, the tears eased, and at last the policewoman prompted her.

'Tell me about Sharon,' she said.

'She's the girl that bunged a stone at me and nearly lost my kite.' Ben thought police intervention was long overdue.

His remarks seemed so inappropriate. Joanne felt older, wiser.

'I don't know her other name,' she said. 'She's this girl. I don't know how old. Twelve, I think. She ran away from her home, in London. And she's in an old shack. Here. In the woods.'

The policewoman nodded.

'When did you meet her?' Mum's voice was soft.

'Last weekend.'

'You should have told us.'

'And she smashed our windscreen,' muttered Ben.

The policewoman put the crumpled piece of paper back in her pocket. 'I think I need to see this Sharon. Will you take me to this shack?'

'We'll all come,' said Mum. 'Get your macs, you two. How far is it, Jo?'

'Not far,' said Joanne. 'It's on the way to the castle.'

'I've got a car,' said the policewoman. 'Can we drive there?'

Joanne nodded. At least they could drive most of the way.

They left the caravan, Dad locking it behind him. Joanne wanted to run, but had to be satisfied with the brisk pace set by the policewoman. They reached the car park, crammed into the police car, and set off.

It was still raining. The policewoman seemed to know the area well, and avoided most of the bumps and potholes when they reached the Ridgeway.

'How far now?'

Joanne pointed to the left. 'Not far,' she said. 'Over the field. There's the wood. That's where the shack is.'

The policewoman stopped the car.

'I think we'll walk from here. Up at the station they get very put out if you bust the suspension on one of their cars.'

They got out. The policewoman took a torch from the dashboard, and then spoke quietly into her radio for a couple of minutes.

Come on, come on – Joanne was saying to herself. Let's get it all over. Quickly.

There was no conversation as they trudged along the sodden path. The policewoman's torch lit up the worst puddles, but it was hard going.

Joanne wondered what state Sharon would be in. Had she got any source of light in the shack? Was she in total darkness? What would Sharon say when they all arrived? With the police! What would she do? Run off? Start a fight? Pull her knife? Joanne wondered if she should warn the policewoman about that knife – in case something terrible happened.

Silly – something terrible *had* happened.

The first sign that something unexpected, as well as terrible, had happened, was spotted by the policewoman when they reached the edge of the field. She shone her torch on tyre-tracks, clearly visible in the soft, wet mud. Even though the bottoms of the ruts were already under water, it was obvious that the tracks were recent, and that there were two sets of them.

'Someone's been along here this evening,' said the policewoman. 'Coming and going.' Her voice sounded puzzled.

They followed the tracks into the wood. Here and there, at the edges of the path, were other signs – flattened grass, and a few branches snapped from trees and bushes.

It was very dark, and quiet save for the pattering of the rain.

The tyre tracks led them straight to the clearing, and there was the hut. Sharon's shack. Long, grubby, disintegrating. Sharon's new home. Soaked by the heavy rain. Dimly lit by the policewoman's torch. The absurdity, the madness, the misery of Sharon's plan was revealed.

Again, Joanne felt relieved. Surely, Sharon would be pleased to see them.

'Hang on a minute.' The policewoman turned away from them and spoke into the radio fastened to the lapel of her jacket. Joanne couldn't hear what she was saying, but it sounded like a request of some sort.

She didn't see the point of waiting. Why not go into the hut *now*, and get Sharon out? Arrest her, if that's what was supposed to happen. Anything. But get Sharon to a safe, warm, dry, bright place. That was what mattered.

The policewoman turned back towards them.

'I think you'd better wait here. They're going to send another officer from Rye. It won't take long.' She smiled, but without conviction. 'This is the hut where Sharon was living?'

Joanne nodded. She didn't like the phrase 'was living'. Her fears that something had gone badly wrong intensified. The policewoman suspected something, and wanted to keep them out of the hut. Joanne assumed the policewoman's fears were her own. That they would find Sharon, dead, on the floor of the hut, among her empty tins and old packets of food.

The policewoman shone her torch around.

'Did your friend Sharon smoke?'

Joanne thought. It was possible, she supposed, but she had never seen Sharon with a cigarette.

'I don't think so,' she said.

'Well, somebody around here does.' The policewoman shone her torch directly on the ground, a little way in front of them. There were several cigarette ends, wet and crushed, on the short grass.

She spoke into her radio once more. Then she said: 'I'll go and have a look at that hut. But you stay here.'

Joanne watched the woman walk to the shack and enter.

Something had gone very wrong.

She could wait no longer. She ran. She heard her father call to her to come back, but took no notice. Her feet slipping on the sodden turf, she raced to the shack. She wrenched the door open, and almost fell in. The policewoman's torch flashed round at her, and she heard a gasp of surprise.

'I told you to wait,' said the policewoman, fiercely.

'Is she dead?' The question had to be asked.

'She isn't here. But somebody's certainly *been* here. And it looks like there's been a fight.'

As the torchlight flickered over the inside of the hut, Joanne saw snatched details, like a magic lantern show. The smashed window. Broken glass on the floor. A cupboard door hanging on its hinges. A brightly coloured beach towel with muddy bootmarks on it. More broken glass. The neck of a bottle. Carboard boxes that looked as though they'd been kicked from end to end of the carriage.

And the pathetic, lifeless form of Sharon's teddy.

Chapter Twenty

They didn't kill her. Her back was sore, her head was pounding – but they didn't kill her. They grabbed her viciously by her bruised arms, and bundled her out into the pouring rain. She was rushed to the van and thrown in the back. Two of her attackers clambered in after her. The watcher climbed in the front, and sat next to the driver. Sharon couldn't be sure, but she reckoned the driver was Wally.

'Took your time,' she heard him say.

'Don't let's hang about then.'

The van started up, the lights flicked on, and they reversed out of the wood, and then lunged forward, at speed, over the field, and up to the crossroads.

Sharon tried to keep track of where they were going. It wasn't the barns, that was for sure, 'cos they were now bumping along the Ridgeway. The real test would be which way they turned at the main road. Left would mean Hastings, right would mean Rye.

The van slowed. Inside, there was tension. Nobody spoke.

They reached the main road.

The van turned right.

So – it was Rye. And then where? London? Or maybe a south coast port – Folkestone, Dover, Ramsgate. They could be going anywhere. Abroad even. They hadn't killed her, but they could easily be planning to dump her somewhere abroad. Or worse, dump her somewhere halfway between England and abroad.

Despite the pain and the headache, her mind raced. Surely, there was no way they could smuggle her abroad. Not on a ferry. Even for a day trip you have to have them identity cards. You couldn't get out of the country without one of them.

London?

Could be. It was a gang all right. Could well be operating from London. A little of Sharon's spirit returned. If they were driving to London, maybe there'd come a chance to bunk it from the van. At traffic lights. Wait for the moment, and then leg it like hell, screaming for help. Wait till they got where there were lights, and people.

Wait? It was all she could do. It was up to this lot of thugs what happened next. For the first time in nine days someone else was looking after her.

The van accelerated down the main road. They reached the outskirts of Rye. The van had no side windows, but there were small windows in the doors at the back, through which Sharon got the occasional glimpse of street lights, houses, shops, cafes. And there were people about, too. It couldn't be all that late.

The van stopped at a road junction. For a moment, Sharon was able to make out a little of the inside of the van. A bundle of rags, and the two heavy-looking men guarding her. Hard, tough, unfriendly.

One thing she couldn't see – any handles on the insides of the back doors. So much for her plan to hop out. She'd never get the doors open.

But there was something else in the back of the van. A pile of footballs.

She pointed to them. 'Where we goin'? Wembley?'

'Shut up!' One of the heavyweights made as if to give her a back-hander. Sharon winced in anticipation of the blow to her face, but he did no more than threaten.

They left Rye, but not by the London road. Sharon vaguely remembered her way round Rye from the old days with Neddie. No, this wasn't the way to London. This was the coast road. They crossed the river. The tide was high, and she could see fishing boats and cabin cruisers moored along the banks.

More speed for a mile or so, and then the van slowed. Where now?

Another right turn. She tried to picture a map in her mind. Where was Wally taking them? Camber? Must be. This was the road to Camber Sands, and there was Rye, receding in the distance.

One of the heavyweights said: 'Taking a risk, aren't you?'

She didn't hear a reply.

The van pulled into the deserted car park at the end of the lane to Camber Sands, splashing through the puddles on the tarmac. Wally switched off the lights.

Slowly, carefully, with the engine merely ticking over, Wally drove through the car park, down the soft slope of sand, and on to the beach.

Sharon could hear the pounding of waves above the engine. She wondered, for a moment, if they were going to drive into the sea, like Chitty-Chitty Bang-Bang, but Wally swung the wheel over and headed along the beach, between the sea and the dunes, back towards the mouth of the river. It wasn't easy for the tyres to grip, and their progress over the mile or so was slow. But, eventually, in the dark and the rain, the van came to a halt at the foot of the dunes, facing the sea, and only a stone's throw from the spot where Joanne and Ben had played 'orphans' one week earlier.

Chapter Twenty-One

The policewoman was abrupt.

'I want Sharon's description. Every detail you can remember.'

Joanne did her best, stumbling over height and weight, and racking her brains to recall what Sharon had been wearing. Dimly, she heard the noise of a car approaching at speed, coming across the field with no regard for suspension. The car stopped. Doors slammed. Voices. More torches. Two policemen, one of them a sergeant.

Joanne gabbled out more of the story, wondering what sense her listeners would make of it. She described the stone-throw, the chase, Wally and the motor-bike, the barns.

'What barns?'

'Wally? Who's he?'

'Why did he chase you?'

No notebooks – the police were in far too much of a hurry. Joanne pointed in the direction of the barns, and gulped something about 'dogs' and 'tape-recorders'.

'Right,' said the police sergeant.

It was like firing the gun at the start of a race. Out of the shack. Back to the trees.

'You'd better come with us,' said the sergeant. 'The rest of your family can follow. But we want to get to these barns of yours, quick.' He looked at Dad. 'That all right with you, sir? We'll see she gets in no danger.'

Dad's mouth opened and shut again, but he was given no time to argue.

They helped Joanne into the back seat of the police car, the two policemen leapt into the front, and they were off, clipping on their seat-belts as they went.

'Hold tight.'

Joanne bounced wildly in the back seat as they accelerated up the path, over the field and back to the crossroads. They passed the policewoman's car and swung left, at Joanne's direction, heading for the barns.

The sergeant swore, and the car braked violently, almost throwing Joanne to the floor. The other policeman flung open his door and ran forward to unfasten a large metal gate that blocked their way. They started up again, and he jumped in while they were going.

The shingle and grass track was only just wide enough for the car, and several times, as they swayed along, Joanne was convinced the car would overturn into the field at the side.

But they reached the barns.

'You stay here and wait for the WPC. She'll be along in a second. But you wait here. Understand?'

No waiting for an answer. Already they were running to the barns.

Lights in the driving mirror. The policewoman's car. Wasting no time. It drew up behind her, and Mum, Dad, Ben and the policewoman scrambled out.

'OK?' said the policewoman.

'They said to wait inside.'

'We all will,' said the policewoman. 'No point in getting even wetter.'

More questions. Wally's description? Joanne couldn't help. She'd never seen his face. More confessions. The secret shopping trips to The Stores. More tears. The windscreen. Dad didn't understand. Joanne couldn't explain.

The sergeant came back. The policewoman wound down the window of the car, and he leaned in.

'There's something going on,' he said. 'A lot of boxes and spuds – all innocent. But there's a whole lot of wiring, bits of plastic, and a couple of loudspeakers.'

'Did you find the football?' asked Ben.

'Football?'

'Wally had a football.'

The sergeant frowned. 'Sounds like a nursery rhyme,' he said.

'And so did the man on the sands. But he threw his football into the sea.'

'Make any sense to you?' the sergeant asked the policewoman.

She shook her head. 'Any sign of the girl?'

There was a shout from the barns.

'Dave! Over here!'

The sergeant withdrew his head from the car, and ran back to his colleague. They both disappeared inside the shed.

More questions. Had Sharon ever talked about anyone else? Anywhere else? Any plans?

Joanne had a question of her own.

'Do you think she's all right?'

'We can't be sure,' said the policewoman. 'Let's hope so.'

'What do you think's happened to her?'

No time for an answer to that one. The two policemen came racing back from the shed. The sergeant had a small polythene bag in his hand. He held it out to the policewoman.

'What do you make of this?'

There was a small slit at one end of the bag. From the bag, the policewoman carefully tipped a tiny amount of white powder. It looked like salt. She sniffed the powder, then licked her finger, dipped it in the powder, and, very cautiously, put a little on her tongue.

Joanne had seen enough television cops-and-robbers programmes to know what was happening. They were testing for drugs.

The policewoman wiped the powder off her tongue, and gave the polythene bag back to the sergeant.

'I'm no expert,' she said, 'but heroin, at a guess.'

The sergeant looked at Ben. 'Footballs, wires, printed circuits, and drugs,' he said.

'And a missing girl,' said the policewoman.

'And a missing girl. This'll wake them up at Hastings. Give 'em a chance to play with the computer at Lewes. Looks like it's going to be a busy night.'

As he reached for the car radio, he looked up at the sky.

'Good job it's stopped raining,' he said.

Chapter Twenty-Two

By craning her neck, Sharon could see through the windscreen. She could make out the sea, and guessed that the tide was nearly as high as it would go. She could also see and hear that it was still raining hard, and could feel the van shake, as the wind buffeted it. As far as she could tell, the beach was empty.

She was alone with a gang of four men. What they were doing, she hadn't a clue. Up to no good, though, that was certain sure. And prepared to smash anyone getting in their way – the pain in her back, her head, and her arms proved that. Whatever they were up to, it must be pretty bad, because they were running one hell of a risk – grabbing her from the shack, kidnapping her, and driving off to the beach like this.

If only some kind copper would come wading out of the sea. Some bold *gendarme*, just finished a quick cross-Channel swim. French coppers carried guns. Need a gun to deal with this lot.

But Sharon wasn't really feeling perky or bright. She was frightened, more frightened than she had ever been in her life, and more frightened than she wanted to admit to herself.

For a long time, in the darkness of the van, nobody spoke.

Sharon broke the silence.

'Anyone fancy a game of cards?'
No answer.
'Football?'
Again, no answer.
''Ow about a paddle?'
From the front came Wally's voice.
'Shut him up.'
'Charming,' said Sharon, in a mocking voice, a split second before a large, hard hand caught her a searing blow on the side of her face.

She'd been hit many times in her life. But she couldn't remember it ever being so savage or so powerful before. She shrank back into the corner of the van and kept quiet, nursing her face and blinking back the tears.

An hour passed.

There were infrequent snatches of conversation between members of the gang. Short, clipped phrases.

'Bloody asking for trouble. Changing plans like this.'
'You got a better idea?'
'More than one kid, you said.'
'You kept watch.'
'No one else near that hut all afternoon.'
'How much longer are we waiting?'
'We're waiting for the tide.'
'I know that! How much longer?'
'Longer than we planned.'
'That's the brat's fault.'
'Bloody madness – rushing things.'
'Like I said – you got a better idea?'
'Risk like this . . .'
'And no come-back once we've got rid of the stuff.'
'What? Dump it?'

'Relax. There's no way anyone can trace it back to us.'

'Except through the brat.'

'Deal with him later.'

'This isn't any old cosh-and-run job.'

'Relax. We'll do it properly.'

'And the brat?'

'Deal with him later.'

That phrase – deal with him later – so simple, so certain. So full of menace, but uttered in Wally's mild, throwaway voice, as though he was talking about making someone a sandwich.

Sharon's fears grew. Silently, she prayed for a rescue, but doubted that she'd get one. Nobody knew where she was. Only Jo and Ben. And they were seventy miles away. In London. Where she should be. With Jim. Letting him look after her.

'You checked the circuits?'

It was the watcher, over his shoulder, to the two men in the back.

'Every one.'

'All right?'

'Course they are.'

'And the floats?'

'Yeah.'

'Put the sugar in?'

'Yeah. And we've set the signals.'

'Let's get rid of them now.'

'We wait for the tide.'

'Releasing them all at once?'

'Right.'

'That's another risk.'

'You fancy driving down here every day for a fortnight? Doing it one at a time?'

'OK, OK.'

'You gonna tell that brat everything?'

That was Wally, with a steely authority behind his soft voice, that brought the others to silence.

Sharon was sweating with fright. She didn't know all the details, but one or two things were obvious. The gang were smuggling something, sending it out in footballs, by sea, with some kind of signal to whoever was waiting for it. The something, whatever it was, was worth a lot of money. It didn't take a genius to think of drugs. And, with so much at stake, it didn't take a genius to realise that the gang would hardly welcome a witness to what was happening.

They hadn't killed her – yet. But it might only be a matter of time.

Rescue? No way. Beg for mercy? Fat chance. Escape? Seemed impossible, but more likely than rescue or mercy.

All right then, how you going to escape?

Got to get out of the van. Once out of the van, there was a chance of legging it. She could run, and the two men in the back with her were a couple of fatties. If she could get a bit of a start, make for the dunes, there was a possibility. But she'd have to get a bit of a start first.

She remembered a stunt she'd pulled more than once in her life. The old toilet dodge. It worked at The Laurels. It worked at Rowandale. It worked at school. Maybe it would work here.

'Gotta go to the toilet.'

There was no response.

Well, at least they hadn't clouted her. She tried to keep the shakes out of her voice.

'Gotta go to the toilet.'

'Shut up.'

She waited a couple of minutes.

'I 'ave. Really. I gotta go to the toilet.'

'You hold it.'

'I can't. I gotta go.'

'You hold it.'

'All right,' said Sharon. 'I'll wee in your van. See 'ow you like that.'

Crack! Another slap across the face.

'Let him go.'

The blow had come from one of the two fatties, but the words came from Wally.

'Supposing he bunks it?'

'One of you can get out with him.'

'It's raining!'

'Then get wet. Get out and get wet. And watch him.'

'Why can't he do it out the back of the van?'

'Because I'm a girl,' said Sharon.

The fatty groaned. 'That's all we need,' he said.

For the first time, Wally turned his head, and stared into the back of the van.

'Get out and watch *her*,' he said.

The fatty did as he was told. The watcher came round from the front and opened the back doors of the van. While Sharon clambered out with her guard, the watcher returned to his seat next to Wally.

Sharon flopped on to the sand.

'Come on. Quick. Round the side. And no messing about.'

He shoved her to the side of the van, and stood there, within an arm's length of her.

That was no good, she'd never get a start that way.

'I ain't going with you lookin',' said Sharon.

'Oh, yes, you are.'

'I ain't.' She stared up at him, as bravely as she could.

She began to squat down, but, as soon as she was certain he wasn't going to turn round, she dropped full-length on the sand, and rolled under the van. Her plan was to run from the other side of the van, giving her an extra second or two before 'Fatty' realised which way she'd gone.

It worked.

Once clear of the van, she sprang to her feet and was away, racing for all she was worth, away from the van, away from the sea, darting over the sand, heading for the dunes.

Silently she counted each lightning pace, speeding the count to speed her legs.

One, two, three, four, five, six, seven, eight . . . one-two-three-four-five-six-seven-eight . . .

There was a shout from behind.

Cursing. Another shout. She heard the van engine start.

Quick, quick, quick. Must reach the dunes. Faster, faster, oh please, faster . . .

Heart pounding, head pounding, coughing, gasping – Sharon forced every tiny impulse of speed from her limbs.

Just once she risked a glance over her shoulder.

Two of them. Coming after her. The two fatties.

There was a chance. The van was turning, but she was almost at the dunes. There was no way they could drive the van up the dunes. They'd have to go right along the beach, back to the car park, and then down the road to catch her. All of two miles.

She reached the dunes.

Bleedin' 'ell!

It was like the ground opening up beneath her. The soft slopes and pits of sand, shifting under each foot-fall. A nightmare to run on, as though her feet were made of lead. Impossible to maintain any sort of pace. They'd get her, surely to God they'd get her.

She dragged her swaying, stumbling body up to the level of the marram grass. That was better to run on, but painful. The whippy stems of the grass stung her legs through her thin jeans. Each step was now a torture.

But she had to ignore that. She was making better progress.

Another glance over her shoulder.

The fatties were doing even worse on the dunes than she had.

The top of the dunes. The van had sped off, down the beach. She gave herself the luxury of two, three gulps of air, taking in the sweet rain as she did so. Then on, tumbling down the land side of the dunes – falling, rolling, struggling up, tumbling again.

A fence. She ran slap into it, and bounced off the netting like it was an upright trampoline. She grabbed the chain-links, and hoisted herself over.

More sand?

No, grass. Grass under her feet. That was more like it. Short grass, too. Chance to put on more speed.

But her feet hurt and her legs hurt and her lungs hurt. And she had no idea where she was.

The river.

She must get back to the river. There'd be people there. Must be. The river. Where Neddie used to take her. Even at this hour, there'd be someone there. Must be!

Sharon fell headlong into some kind of pit.

Not more sand? No, it wasn't a pit. A bunker. This must be the golf-course.

She got back to her feet and staggered on, but she wasn't moving at much of a speed now. She'd already covered the best part of a mile, and her strength was beginning to fail.

And then, suddenly, it stopped raining, and she could see the river-bank ahead. And lights.

One two three four five six seven eight . . . one . . . two . . . three . . . four . . . five . . .

She reached the river. The lights were to her right, inland. Below her, the water was starting to flood out, at the turn of the tide.

She stood for a moment on the bank, and looked behind her. She couldn't be sure, but she thought she could see signs of movement, back on the golf-course. The fatties, in hot pursuit.

She headed inland, along the river-bank, making for the lights, which she guessed must be Rye Harbour.

The boat station! That was on this side of the river! There'd be people there.

But she never got to the boat station.

She saw it distinctly enough, but she also saw something else.

The watcher.

Wally must have dropped him off from the van. The van had beaten her to it. They had outsmarted her.

And the watcher began to move swiftly towards her.

Chapter Twenty-Three

'It's a waste of time,' said Jim, angrily. 'Wild-goose chase.'

'What did you expect?' said Carol.

Tension between them had built up on the drive down. Jim had hardly said a word. Wanted a bit of p-and-q, Carol reckoned. Fair enough: but she wasn't going to let him take his disappointment out on her.

'I don't know,' snapped Jim. 'I expected . . . something. Not a load of smart-alec remarks from the locals.'

'Yeah, well, it's a pity we weren't after someone with a more sensible name than Neddie.'

'We might as well go home,' said Jim.

The slipway was deserted. The pub was shut. Lights were on in the boat station across the river, but there were no other signs of life. It had stopped raining, but the sky was heavily overcast. The wind, gusting over the salt marshes, rocked the boats at their moorings.

Boats.

Hundreds of them. Small craft, many of them so like the one in the photo. But none of them quite right.

There was nothing here. No warmth. No life. Nothing to help you. No one to blame. Wild and wasteful. A bit like Sharon.

Carol shivered. Jim stamped his feet.

'Come on. We might as well go home.'

Carol looked at him out of the corner of her eye. It was going to be a miserable ride back, with a rotten welcome awaiting them at The Laurels. It would be better to delay the return as long as possible. In the hope that all the kids would be in bed, asleep, by the time they returned.

Every few seconds, a mournful hooter sounded from the mouth of the river.

'Oh, come on, Carol . . .'

'What's the point of going back?'

'What's the point of staying here?'

'You give up easy, don't you?'

The words were meant to hurt. And they did.

'No, I don't give up easy. I go on and on, bashing my head against a brick wall, long after it's clear it will do no good. That's why I'm still trying to make plans for Sharon. That's why I'm down here – on this bloody wild-goose chase!'

'Sharon isn't a wild-goose. She's a silly cow.'

'All right, all right. Look, we're both tired. We've come down here, ready to do our great rescue act, and she isn't here. Let's go home. Please.'

'I hate giving up,' said Carol.

'I know.'

'You do give up easy. You gave up searching her room.'

'Yes, yes.'

'You gonna give up The Laurels? You gonna let that fat old Mrs B close the place?'

'I . . .'

'You better not! You gonna give up helping Sharon?'

'Helping her? She doesn't give me a chance!'

'There you go. Giving up.'

'Carol, it's late. It's cold. I'm tired. We're both tired.'

From the river-mouth came the mocking call of the hooter. It was the last straw for Jim.

'Carol!' He started walking to the car.

She didn't move.

'Carol, please! I've got some chocolate in the car.'

Big deal! What a bribe! Still – why not?

Carol clattered after him.

They turned their backs on the river, so they didn't see Sharon arrive on the opposite bank, a couple of hundred metres downstream. They didn't see her stagger, stumble on the planks of the jetty, tumble down a ladder and drop into a dinghy. Nor did they see the fatties, hurrying after her. Nor the watcher, closing in from the direction of the boat station.

Instead, they sat in the car and ate chocolate.

When they had finished, Jim reached forward and turned on the ignition.

'I still think you give up too easy,' said Carol.

Chapter Twenty-Four

The watcher had seen her. There was no doubt about that, and there was nowhere she could hide. Behind her, the two fatties were closing up fast.

She was no swimmer. The river looked dark, oily, deep, cold, swirling. A boat. That was what she needed. Quick – a boat.

There were dozens of them. Which one? Any one. Nearest.

Heart thumping, legs trembling, Sharon tottered along the jetty. She felt hot and cold at the same time: hot from the frantic efforts of her flight, and cold from the bite of the wind on her soaking clothes. Her shaking hands fumbled for the top of one of the ladders that led straight down from the jetty to the boats and water below. Even at this moment of panic, she recalled Neddie's instructions: 'Always go down backwards'. She clambered down, and fell into a small dinghy, scraping her backbone on one of the thwarts.

She ignored the pain, and half bounced and half hauled herself up and felt about her. Oars – surely there'd be oars!

She couldn't find them.

Never mind the oars. Got to bleedin' cast off first.

She was momentarily out of sight of the watcher and

the others, but she could hear their footsteps, stomping on the planks above.

Her little pink hands grasped the thick wet rope that fastened the dinghy to the piling.

What a knot! The size of her hand and as hard as rock. There was no way she'd loosen that. Her fingers slipped off again and again as she tore helplessly at the harsh folds.

Cut it! Cut it! She'd forgotten her knife. All that time. Stuck in her sock. She snatched it and hacked at the knot.

Nitwit! Leave the knot, cut the single strand.

'Down here!'

A voice almost directly above.

She stabbed, sliced, sawed at the rope, terrified that she wouldn't have sufficient strength. Then, she felt the strands of the rope parting.

She was through.

Shove off. God help us, there was a leg already on the ladder, and a foot poised like it was about to stamp on her upturned face.

Sharon threw herself to the side of the dinghy and pushed as hard as she could against the piling. Helped by the steadily increasing current of the outgoing tide, the dinghy swung round, and away.

She heard a filthy oath spat at her from the ladder, but the dinghy had moved far enough for the vicious kick to miss her head.

She'd got to get across.

No oars? Then paddle with your hands.

It was wild work. With her arm fully extended over the side, and the gunwales of the boat cutting into her armpit, her hand could still barely reach the water. She clawed at the surface, and then lurched to the other side of the dinghy, trying to keep the nose of the boat pointing across the river.

At first she made no progress. It was like another nightmare: where the faster you run, the slower you move. The boat drifted towards the river-mouth, towards the sea. All the time she expected to feel a hand on her shoulder, dragging her back to the side.

She glanced round.

It was tiny, the distance between her and the piling. There was the watcher, staring down at her, but the two fatties had moved downstream, and were slowly descending another ladder.

Another boat. They'd be after her in a moment. And you could bet they'd make a better job of crossing.

Don't think about that. Don't think about *anything*. Keep your hands going, your arms going, the boat going. Got to get across. Got to. Get across and make for the pub, the houses. And all the time, the tide was carrying her the wrong way.

Sharon fought, slapped, churned her way across the river. Halfway . . . three-quarters . . . a few more suffering, agonising pulls with her arms. She'd do it! Surely she'd do it!

There. There. The other bank. Bleak, dark, harsh. Sharon stretched out her cold, numbed hands, and hardly noticed the pain as the rough concrete tore the skin from her knuckles. She grasped a rusty metal ring, embedded in the concrete, and hauled herself out of the boat, her legs dangling and dipping in the water, as the tide wrenched the dinghy from under her.

The Shack by the Sea

She was some way from the pub. But the fatties would have a job getting ashore, with any luck.

Trouble was, she was almost done. Her shoulder hurt, her back hurt, her leg hurt, even her teeth hurt. And, as the feeling returned to her hands, they, too, hurt. She was a mass of limping, aching bruises. Somehow she kept going. She had to get to the pub, to the houses. Ring a bell, beat on a door. Scream. Anything. Just get someone's attention. Get someone to notice her. To see here was Sharon. Alive, only just, but alive and needing help.

Another hundred metres. Fifty. She gulped a deeper breath to start calling, shouting, shrieking.

Too late.

No. No, no, no.

Wally's van, smashing into the car park, and Wally leaping out. He must have sussed out she'd cross the river, and here he was to finish her off at the last moment.

For a second, Sharon stopped. Only her head moved, swivelling this way and that, looking hopelessly for escape.

Behind her – the fatties. On the opposite bank – the watcher. Ahead of her – Wally. To the side – the deep, flooded gravel pits.

But there was a nearer, darker shape. Like an ancient, crumbling wedding-cake. Derelict, unwelcoming, but solid and safe. The martello tower.

And to the tower Sharon ran.

She remembered the window, the ivy, the bushes, the broken bricks and half ledges, all of which would give her footholds. Despite exhaustion, she still reckoned she was more nimble than Wally and the fatties would ever be. Years of bunking it had given her confidence in her own agility.

The worst bit was the sloping, slithering clamber up the shingle slope. With every step, the stones rolled away from beneath her feet, forcing her to climb on all fours to keep her balance. The cuts on her hands deepened, and, though she didn't know it, she left little drops of blood on the stones as she scrambled along. With that climb, though only a few metres, the last measures of survival evaporated from her body.

Almost crawling, she reached the handrail at the top of the slope, clung to it, and dragged herself to her feet. She could see and hear Wally and the fatties stamping up the shingle below her.

Then came the certain physical knowledge that she simply couldn't run any further. She must stop. Lie down. Sleep. Just find a hole to worm into. No time. No light. No energy.

She did the only thing left for her to do, and rolled over the edge of the parapet, snatching with arms and legs in the hope of catching something that would break her fall.

She was lucky. A stout elder bush, and some old, gnarled ivy, saved her. She swung, slipped, grabbed, swung again, and finally bumped to the bottom.

She was in the moat that surrounded the tower. For a while, she lay on the soft, wet grass – breathless, and twitching with distress, but relieved to find that she still wanted to be alive. Ten metres above her, Wally and the fatties appeared at the handrail; hot, bothered, and apparently uncertain as to how they could get her.

But it could only be a matter of time before they found a way down.

Sharon rose to her knees and peered up at the tower. From the bottom of the moat it looked impossibly tall. What was it she'd said to Ben: 'Don't fancy 'avin' to climb that'? No – but she had to, now. One of the windows. Get up there and stay up there. None of them could follow her up there. And, if they tried, she'd crack their heads open with stones and loose bricks.

Wearily, she began her climb up the steep face of the tower. There were footholds, but you couldn't trust all of them. The hectic chase had suddenly slowed to sluggish suspense. The gang were searching for a way down into the moat. She could hear them arguing, swearing. She spared a moment to turn her head towards them. Wally was standing there, staring across at her, gripping the handrail.

Yeah, though Sharon, 'opin' I'll slip and kill meself.

Slowly. Carefully. One step at a time. A brick broke under one foot, and she had to swing her weight violently back to her other foot to save herself from falling. She tried again, testing for a better hold. There . . . lean across . . . now, the other side . . . feeling . . . feeling . . . feeling with her foot until she knew it was safe. She risked a look upwards. There was the window, still some way off, but she had climbed over half way. Take it careful, and she'd make it.

Crack!

Christ! What was that?

Crack! Crack!

Stones. Smashing into the wall above her, below her, all around her. Splintering, ricocheting, bouncing.

They were stoning her. Bastards! Bastards!

She almost lost her grip in terror at what would happen if the stones hit her.

The fusillade increased. Wally was directing, urging the others. The stones crashed into the tower, bringing down chips of brick and mortar, some of which fell on her.

But the moat was wide, and, in the darkness, the gang's aim was poor.

She reached the window. There was a wide ledge, more than big enough for her to sit on, and plenty strong enough to support her. Here she perched, safe from falling, out of the wind, and almost completely protected from the stones rattling around her. She slumped down, not knowing what would happen next, and incapable of further thought or effort.

It was this, or nothing.

And then, all hell broke loose.

Chapter Twenty-Five

Joanne lost track of all the police messages. The radio exchanges were brief, staccato, question and answer. Occasionally, the sergeant would tell them what was happening.

'Hastings are on to it now. Sending a couple of Granadas . . . Something on the go out at Camber Sands . . . A van on the beach . . . Trying to get hold of a sniffer-dog.'

Then came the message that really mattered.

'Chap out at Rye Harbour's reported a youth cutting loose a boat. Men in pursuit. Sounds a right old racket. Could be your friend,' he said to Joanne. 'They're contacting the harbour-master.'

'What do they want us to do?' asked the policewoman.

'They don't seem sure.'

If the police didn't seem sure, Joanne did. She was going to the harbour. Not in the car, that would take too long, going back all the way they had come, and then right round by the road – seven or eight miles. Here they were, less than a mile from the harbour. Only a step or two from the spot where Sharon had cut Ben's kite-string.

'I wanted to see what would happen if it was free.'

Sharon's words. Standing here. Knife in hand. A little out of breath, but four-square, facing her accusers. No remorse. No weakness. But now, a week later, Joanne heard the words differently. A tiny hope in them, that someone would understand what it was all about. The stone-throwing. The smashing. Hiding. Running away.

'Could be your friend,' the sergeant had said.

You bet it was. And men after her. Someone had better step in quickly. Before . . .

No need for further thoughts, and no time for them, either.

Joanne ran, flying over the narrow path through the fields, to Rye Harbour.

She could hear car doors slamming behind her, but others pounding after her, on foot. Reassured, Joanne sped on. The path widened to a grass track, narrowed again by the builder's yard, and she was on the lane leading to Rye Harbour.

A few dim street lights, obscured by chestnuts and hawthorns, bordering the road. Eerie shadows, but homely lights in some of the upstairs windows. More lights ahead, where the lane ended at the car park by the pub. More lights and noises. Shouting. People pointing.

Joanne ran past them, but stopped abruptly when she saw what they were pointing at. Figures, at the top of the slope, by the martello tower. Figures in aggressive movement, vicious and violent.

A fight.

Jim hadn't even got as far as releasing the handbrake when Wally's van screeched into the car park and smashed into their offside wing.

'What the hell!'

Jim put all his weight on the car horn.

Lights were switched on in the houses.

Wally leapt from his van and raced to the tower. Jim wasn't going to let a hit and run driver get away with that. He was out of the car and off like a bullet. Carol, trembling a little with shock, struggled after him.

The van-driver was making for some old tower, with Jim in hot pursuit. There seemed to be others involved. Two more men. There were shouts. Sounded like a quarrel.

Carol arrived at the bottom of the slope of stones that led up to the tower. The voices and noises came from above.

Up there.

God Almighty, what was going on!

Stones.

The three men, the van-driver and the two others. Hurling stones at something. At the tower. At the window. Across the ditch.

Bloody hooligans!

And there was Jim, bellowing with rage, and about to attack them. Why?

Carol's eyes flicked, like disco lights, from Jim, to the men, to the window.

There was something there.

Someone!

A little figure, perched on the ledge, pressing back into the shadows, sheltering, cowering from the missiles that clattered around her.

Sharon.

No wonder Jim was charging at them. Carol saw the first hooligan wait for Jim to get close, and then aim a scything kick. But the man overbalanced on the shifting stones as his leg swung, and he fell heavily. Jim left him, and raced to the next hooligan.

Carol heard one of them call out: 'Leave him. Get to the van!'

Two of them brushed past Jim, shoving him as they went, and barging him into the handrail. The impact jarred Jim's whole body, and, for a second or two, he pirouetted like a drunken ballet dancer.

They were getting away. The hooligans. No matter. Sharon. Where was Sharon? Still up at the window? Carol couldn't see.

Had she fallen?

No. Still there.

Lights, sirens, shouts, screams, doors slamming. Everything happening down below, back in the car park. Police cars. Lots of them. And one hell of a fight.

But somebody had better get to Sharon.

Carol scrambled up the slope and joined Jim.

He was standing on the edge of the deep ditch, peering across to Sharon. The gap seemed immense.

'Sharon! It's me, Jim.'

He had called across roads, parks, fields, shopping precincts. This time it was a moat.

'Sharon!' He called louder.

There was a slight, trembling movement in the aperture. A piece of ledge dropped off and fell into the moat below.

'Stay there. Don't move, love. Stay there.'

Carol knew he was trying to make his words sound steady, calming – but it was difficult against the background furore from below.

'I'm going to wait here with you. We'll get someone to bring a ladder. So that we can get you down. OK? Just wait there. Won't be long. Promise.'

At the word 'promise', he got an answer from the ledge.

'Jim.'

It was neither cry nor question. Merely a tiny recognition. She knew him. She heard his voice. She accepted his promise. The years of holding her, restraining her, arguing with her, laughing with her, not giving up, paid their dividend. He was Jim, the one person who kept his promise. It was enough. She said no more, but listened as his voice told her what was going to happen.

The gap was bridged.

Steps hurried up the shingle.

A girl, and a smaller child, a boy. A policewoman.

'Carol's here with me.'

Jim talked on, about where the car was parked, and they'd got the rug in it, and she could wrap up warm and snug, with the heater on, and the radio, and the three of them would drive back to The Laurels. Carol would make her a hot drink – milk and honey. And she could have a bath. And then they'd tuck her up in bed, and she could rest. And sleep. And tell them all about this in her own good time.

Nobody else spoke.

When the police and harbour-master arrived with ladders, they tip-toed past Jim, so that every word he uttered should be heard.

But, as their torches swept to and fro, lighting up one face after another, Joanne saw the tears slipping down Jim's cheeks, and Carol heard the break in his voice.

Later

They were sorting everything out.

It would take weeks, the police said, to collect all the evidence to bring Wally and the fatties to trial. And they were mighty sorry not to have got hold of the watcher – who had slipped away from the far side of the river.

Still, they had got the rest of the gang. And the drugs.

It was a member of the drug squad who explained everything to Joanne and Ben.

'Good scheme,' he said. 'You put packets of heroin into plastic footballs and chuck them into the sea.'

'But they could go anywhere,' said Ben.

'No. Each football had a little bleeper. That's what the wiring was all about. Gave off a signal as the football floated out into the Channel, and there was a boat ready, with the receiving equipment. They picked up the footballs, and off they went to Holland, Denmark, wherever the market was for the drugs.'

To Ben's disgust, although the drugs would have fetched millions of pounds, there was no reward. And, to Joanne's disappointment, their parents wanted as little publicity as possible. She had a few days' fame at school – that was all.

Within a very short time she thought she was back to

normal, but, as the dark, wet days passed in November and December, she began to realise that she had changed. The day-dreams had gone. She didn't want to be an orphan. Or a heroine. Or like Lynsey. Or like Vanessa. Or like anyone else. She simply wanted to be more of herself.

She wondered how much of this was down to the mad adventure she and Ben had shared with Sharon. Then she wondered how Sharon was. At Christmas, she sent a card with a letter inside, and, a couple of weeks later, received a reply – from Jim.

Dear Joanne,
Sharon insists she will be writing to you, but I've known people wait a very long time for an answer from Sharon. So, I'm writing on her behalf.
You ask how she is. Well, she's recovered from her ordeal quicker than I have. And she says there won't be any more expeditions (fingers crossed!) It's early days yet, but maybe she's right. She *has* changed. We still get trouble at school, but here, at The Laurels, she's like an angel. Can you believe it? The fostering plan has been cancelled, and she's delighted. You may have read in the local paper that The Laurels will close next year. It does look, however, as though Sharon and I will be able to move together to a new 'Teenage Unit' (horrid phrase!) for our 'special' customers. I must be mad, but I'm almost looking forward to taking Sharon with me.
I'm glad to hear that you and Ben are OK, and not suffering any disastrous consequences from your contact with Sharon.

I'll have another go at persuading her to write.
Take care,
Best wishes,
Jim

In February, a home made Christmas card arrived from Sharon. The picture on the front was of a crudely drawn railway-carriage, with three 'pin' people standing outside, holding Christmas puddings the size of footballs.

Inside was a message.

Remember M
Remember E
Put them together
And remember ME

There was a PS on the back.

Meant to send this yonks ago.
Still – never mind eh? Me and
Jim's moving to a new place.
He says everything's getting
sorted out. Wot a larf!!!!!
Sharon

Mum and Dad seemed to want to regard the whole episode as finished. Ben had nothing to say on the subject. Joanne was left alone with her thoughts.

And, when the family returned to the caravan for a weekend in March, Joanne walked alone to the wood. The shack had gone. There were a few rotting panels of wood and some pieces of broken glass. That was all.

She presumed it had been dismantled and removed. There were no tyre-tracks. No cigarette ends. No sounds of dogs barking. No one threw a stone at her.

But the barns were still there. And the martello tower. It had all been real enough. Something she would never forget. Someone she would never forget.